AN ALLEGHENY TRIUMPH OF JUSTICE

Carrie Williams' Courageous Fight
for Equal Rights
in the Early Jim Crow Era

Kathleen Jackson Costantini

35th Star Publishing
Charleston, West Virginia
www.35thstar.com

Copyright © 2019 by Kathleen Jackson Costantini.
All Rights Reserved.
Printed in the United States of America.

35th Star Publishing
Charleston, West Virginia
www.35thstar.com

No part of this book may be reproduced in any form or in any means, electronic or mechanical, including photocopying, recording, or any information retrieval system, without permission in writing from the publisher.

An Allegheny Triumph of Justice / Kathleen Jackson Costantini -- 1st ed.
ISBN-13: 978-1-7350739-3-4
ISBN-10: 1-7350739-3-8
Library of Congress Number: 2019903873

On the cover: Scenic West Virginia mountains photography by Daniel Friend, used by license through Shutterstock. Front and back cover images of young students are from the Library of Congress. These students were from Pocahontas County, West Virginia, and are representative of the students who benefitted from Carrie Williams' case.

Cover Design by: Studio 6 Sense – www.studio6sense.com

To Tom

Contents

Acknowledgements i
Preface iii
Prologue vii
West Virginia in the Making 1
The Grand Old Man of West Virginia 19
The Miners 45
The Honorable Judge 73
Educator and Protector 89
Civil Rights Advocate and Attorney 111
Carrie Goes to Court 149
Epilogue 185
Bibliography 189
Index 203
About the Author 213

Acknowledgements

I am indebted to so many people who helped me to tell Carrie's story.

First and foremost, I want to thank Tom Sudbrink who not only introduced me to Wild and Wonderful West Virginia, but also has been my steadfast partner on this journey. I am also grateful to my daughter Colleen Cerami-Segal and my son Matt Costantini for their unwavering support and encouragement. In addition, I extend my heartfelt appreciation to Angelina Cerami, Meagan Segal and Kiersten Segal for bolstering my spirits throughout this project.

I would also like to express my gratitude to my sister Meg Tomezak for her staunch encouragement and support. Many thanks to Heather Andrus who never failed to provide much needed heartening assistance. I am also indebted to Tim Tomezak, Greg Tomezak, Richard Segal, Tommie Brink and Tommy Dorian for their encouragement and technical expertise. In addition, I am grateful to Dana Bliss for his considerate and thoughtful counsel. Moreover, I want to thank Lynn Tesher who never failed to provide new ideas and positive reinforcement as I wrote this book. I am also indebted to Corine Fitzpatrick for her consistent support and insightful comments. Furthermore, I appreciate the assistance of Carrie's descendants, Mr. and Mrs. Curtis Smith, for their efforts in accessing family photographs.

I am deeply grateful to so many people in West Virginia for their enthusiastic support as I explored Carrie's narrative. Most importantly, I want to thank Steve Cunningham at 35th Star Publishing for his invaluable and always patient and kind advice in writing this book. Special thanks to Rose Davis, president of the Tucker County Historical Society, for her ready access to materials at the Historical Society's Museum. Most importantly, I am indebted to Connie Eye for her tireless work in locating photographs in the museum's collection. Furthermore, I am grateful to Tom and Judy Rodd at the Friends of Blackwater and the J.R. Clifford Project. Not only have they provided a multitude of resources, but also they have been a generous source of advice throughout this endeavor. Also, a special thank you to Mark Podvia at the West Virginia University College of Law Library for his ready assistance in obtaining key materials for this work. In addition, I extend my heartfelt appreciation to Ryan Gaujot for his all-important aid on the mountain in Douglas, West Virginia.

Finally, I want to acknowledge the West Virginia Division of Culture and History, the Ohio Memory Project, the New York Public Library and JSTOR. Their collective wealth of materials has been an invaluable resource in researching this project.

Preface

An Allegheny Triumph of Justice, Carrie Williams' Courageous Fight for Equal Rights in the Early Jim Crow Era is a celebration of a true American hero. Carrie Williams, the African American teacher at the Coketon Colored School in Tucker County, West Virginia in the 1890s, bravely confronted an attempt to rob black children of their educational rights. Her story is set within the burgeoning Jim Crow era that legally sanctioned black second-class citizenship in the post Reconstruction period and beyond. In 1892 when Carrie received her teaching contract, a contract that as an austerity measure shortened the school term for African American children to five months while retaining an eight-month calendar for white children, she resolved to fight this inequity despite possible adverse consequences for herself and her family. Amid these racially charged times when African Americans experienced meager legal success, Carrie courageously challenged the all-white Tucker County Board of Education in a court of law. Her struggle demonstrates courage, strength, and perseverance as she successfully eradicated an injustice to the African American children in Coketon and ultimately throughout the entire state.

Although the drama of Carrie's successful litigation occurs in West Virginia, the multifaceted issues inherent in her struggle belong to the country as a whole, providing greater insight into the nation's ongoing exploration of what it means to be the Great American Experiment. In many ways, the early history of West Virginia uniquely mirrors the larger social, economic and legal struggles that the United States experienced in this time period as the country grappled with the legacy of slavery and the rapid industrial development of the post Civil War period. When Carrie Williams sued the Board of Education, she challenged not only racial injustice, but also the far-reaching corporate power that the Davis Coal and Coke Company exerted in Tucker County and throughout the state of West Virginia. A deeper understanding of the historical context of the fast changing American landscape of this era heightens an appreciation of both Carrie's bravery and accomplishment.

Carrie's efforts depict the power of the individual to confront injustice and to achieve a truly positive societal impact. Her success in preventing this effort to deprive African American children of their right to a "fair and legal education" (Carrie's words) remained a beacon of hope in the racially stratified America of the protracted Jim Crow era. She is celebrated in this book for her strength of character and her steadfast belief in the possibilities that fairness and justice hold in the American experience despite, at times, evidence to the contrary. Most importantly, Carrie's accomplishment is anchored in her belief in the rule of law that protects the rights of all citizens. She not only prevented a clear injustice in Tucker County, but also set a standard barring the spread of that injustice in West Virginia. Carrie Williams' achievement once again points to the belief that the Great American Experiment rests upon the principle of the equal protection of all citizens under the rule of law.

This is Carrie's story, a true American heroic narrative.

                                        Kathleen Jackson Costantini
                                        June 2019

Prologue

Time and Place: Spring of 1892 in the Coketon Colored School, Coketon, West Virginia

Carrie walked briskly down the gravel path leading to the Coketon Colored School. Opening the door, her eyes scanned the rows of desks neatly arranged before her in the large room of the schoolhouse. As she entered the adjacent room, she placed her shawl on the clothes hook and decided against making a fire in the stove. "Such a beautiful spring day! The sun will keep us all warm today," she thought.

But it wasn't the weather that troubled Carrie that day. Putting her worn school bag on the wooden desk, she sat down and began emptying its contents – carefully graded compositions, pictures from the local gazette, a sandwich and an apple for lunch, and finally, a formal letter from the Tucker County Board of Education of Fairfax District, West Virginia. That letter had *weighed heavily on her mind as she made her way to school earlier that morning.*

Walking down the street where she and the other miner families lived in side-by-side duplex dwellings, she listened to the constant moan of the tipple hard at work sending coal to the waiting railroad cars. As always, she could smell the gas permeated air peppered with coal dust, all bustling signs of the company town hard at work. Gazing at the rushing Blackwater River near the train tracks outside the schoolhouse, Carrie wondered about the children, colored and white, and what their futures would bring.

Opening the envelope, Carrie read again the contract that shortened the school year for black children to five months. She knew all too well that the white children would attend school for the normal eight-month term. Carrie also knew that Coketon and the surrounding area were booming with the enormous financial success of Davis Coal and Coke Company, so why curtail the education of black children in Coketon? More importantly, what could she do to prevent this injustice?

For Carrie, the answer to this question propelled her into action to challenge this inequity despite possible negative repercussions for herself and her family. In her quiet, determined and steady manner, Carrie Williams chose to confront the far-reaching political and economic power of Davis Coal and Coke Company that not only controlled the all-white Tucker County school board, but also embodied the lifeline of the surrounding six towns. Her battlefield was a courtroom and her champion was John Robert Clifford, the first African American lawyer admitted to the bar in West Virginia. Carrie's story exemplifies courage, strength, and perseverance in her quiet, yet highly effective, campaign to eradicate an injustice to her own children, her students and African American children throughout West Virginia. Her efforts depict the power of the individual to confront inequity and to achieve a truly positive societal impact.

While this is a narrative about a strong, young African American woman suing an all-white school board in the burgeoning Jim Crow era, it is also a window into the lives of the people involved as they interact in this unfolding drama of the developing national identity of the United States. Exploring the context of their lives heightens an appreciation of the multifaceted themes present in American history and culture as it impacts the story of Carrie Williams. To some extent, this story, like other real life dramas, is told from the perspectives of the people involved.

Carrie's story is a particularly American narrative, reflective of the ongoing struggle of the United States to define itself and to guarantee full civil rights to all citizens. Created in the turmoil of the Civil War, West Virginia provides a unique mirror into the nation's continuing effort to delineate its values in a rapidly changing world. Although the drama of Carrie's successful challenge occurs in this state, the complex issues inherent in her endeavor belong to the country as a whole, providing greater insight into the nation's exploration of what it means to be the Great American Experiment.

CHAPTER ONE

West Virginia in the Making

In many ways, the history of West Virginia is a microcosm of American politics, economic development and social evolution as the United States sought to define its national identity. More than eighty years after the ratification of the Constitution, the young nation continued to articulate the relationship between the federal government and states' rights. At the same time, Americans eagerly explored an ever-broadening economic destiny as the country moved from an agrarian society to a more industrialized population seeking both national and international marketplaces. Intrinsic to this discourse was the ongoing debate over slavery that had plagued the United States since its inception. As America expanded, so too did the slavery crisis, creating deep societal divisions over the role that the "peculiar institution" played in the nation's development.

Born in the tumult of the American Civil War, the creation of West Virginia tells not only the story of the state's internal conflicts, but also the saga of armed conflict, the debate over the rights of African Americans, the role of new immigrants and the rapidly developing industrialization of the United States. As modern day America emerged in the aftermath of the Civil War, the country embraced the industrial era stimulated by the conflict's demands for arms, equipment and supplies. The rich coalfields and dense timberlands of West Virginia were a treasure trove of natural resources waiting to fuel a nation. Added to this was the necessity of expanding the railroads in order to transport the goods that would transform the country into a national marketplace and an international player in the world economy.

The history of West Virginia from its inception to the heyday of coal mining and timber production provides a penetrating look into the development of the United States as it struggled to define basic American values for all of its citizens. From its initial state constitutional convention in Wheeling throughout the post Civil War period to the turn of the early twentieth century, West Virginia's evolution uniquely mirrors national debates as the United States sought to define itself in a fast changing industrialized era. Inherent in this ongoing evolution are the stories of the self made entrepreneurs of the post Reconstruction era and the men and women who forged communities out of the new mining and timber towns along the fast growing railroad lines of West Virginia. Against the vast, mountainous backdrop of West Virginia, the conflicts implicit in the belief in social Darwinism unfolded as miners struggled to unionize in a time period where federal and state governments all too often aligned themselves with the interests of big business and banking. It is also the narrative of inevitable heightened tensions as miners found themselves engulfed in a dangerous work environment coupled with an equally stifling economic system controlled by the owners of the coal mines.

Intrinsic to this unfolding drama is the ongoing debate about the legacy of slavery and the rights of African Americans in the post Reconstruction period. While the 1872 revised state constitution prohibited racial intermarriage and mandated segregated schools, West Virginia maintained African American male suffrage rights. As southern and former border states of the Civil War period found ways to disenfranchise blacks and relegate them to second-class citizenship through the passage of Jim Crow laws, West Virginia, despite internal conflicts, never deprived African American men of the right to vote. And, as the story of Carrie Williams reveals, African American children in West Virginia were never relegated to a shortened school year or their teachers to lower salaries than their white counterparts.

Threaded into this tapestry of American life is the pervasive belief in the promise that the Great American Experiment holds for all citizens: the possibility of a better life for themselves and their children. The West Virginia mining towns beckoned native Mountaineers, citizens from other states, particularly African Americans seeking opportunities outside of the agrarian impoverishment of the New South, and recent immigrants from southern and eastern Europe, all in pursuit of this promise. An understanding of West Virginia's development into statehood and beyond is a window into the multilayered evolution of the United States as a whole.

On October 16, 1859, when John Brown and his twenty-one followers raided the federal arsenal at Harper's Ferry in what would become part of West Virginia, impending armed conflict loomed over the young nation. Under the overall command of Colonel Robert E. Lee, U.S. Marines from the Marine Barracks in Washington, D.C., led by First Lieutenant Israel Greene recaptured the arsenal and John Brown was subsequently tried and hanged for treason against the Commonwealth of Virginia. With the election of Abraham Lincoln in 1860, the Lower South seceded, and at the convention in Montgomery, Alabama, created a new government, the Confederate States of America. Tensions within the United States escalated rapidly as the country moved perilously close to armed hostilities.

Although the Civil War had not yet officially begun, debate surrounding Virginia's role in the imminent conflict intensified. At the Virginia Convention, later referred to as the Secession Convention, called in February of 1861, many delegates were pro Unionist. However, within two months, political allegiances shifted dramatically after the fall of Fort Sumter and President Lincoln's subsequent call for 75,000 volunteers from all states to suppress the rebellion. These events heightened existing political sectional divisions within the state. Woven into the internal debate in the western section of Virginia were deeply rooted feelings about the relationship of the federal government and states' rights. While some western Virginians believed that their foremost allegiance rested with the Commonwealth, others felt an intense loyalty to the Union and were not afraid to commit that loyalty to action despite the risk to their lives and fortunes.

Added to this contentious dialogue were conflicting views about the future of slavery in the state. Although some argued for the rights of their fellow Virginians to be slave owners, abolition came to dominate this discourse. For many residents, antislavery sentiments were rooted in economics since they believed that slavery diminished opportunities for white laborers, while for others, the abolition of slavery was a moral necessity. Earlier in 1847, Dr. Henry Ruffner advised in *The Ruffner Pamphlet*, "But let all the West, (western Virginia) on due consideration, conclude that slavery is a pernicious institution, and must be gradually removed...." H. Helper further stressed this sentiment in *The Impending Crisis* when he admonished, "Heaven forbid that a desperate faction of slaveholding criminals should succeed in their infamous endeavors to quench the spirit of liberty, which our forefathers infused into those two sacred charters of our political faith, the Declaration of Independence, and the Constitution of the United States."[1] Antislavery sentiments intertwined with an intense loyalty to the Union that superseded allegiance to the Commonwealth soon dominated in western Virginia as the country verged on outright war.

Here, numbers help to describe the complex political and sociological environment of western Virginia. In 1860, the total population of what would become West Virginia was 378,000. Of that number, approximately 21,000 or 5 ½ percent were black, including 2,800 who were free. The African American population was widely scattered: 75 percent lived in the eastern counties of Jefferson, Berkeley, Hampshire and Hardy and the southern counties of Greenbrier, Monroe and Kanawha, while 25 percent lived in the remaining counties. Consequently, the more clustered black population had a greater visibility, helping to explain why some white conservatives were concerned about eventually enfranchising African Americans.[2] Although the black population was widely dispersed, free blacks were vitally involved in the towns, cities and rural areas of what would become West

Virginia. According to historian Connie Park Rice, "The presence of a politically active black community during and immediately following the Civil War refutes not only the myth of a homogeneous white society in Appalachia, but also the myth of a region geographically isolated from the rest of the nation."[3] In 1861, as the Civil War officially commenced, the same part of Virginia that would emerge as West Virginia contributed substantially to both the Union Army and to the Confederate cause, illustrating the conflicting allegiances within the area.[4]

The volatile crisis within Virginia reached a crescendo on April 17, 1861, at the Virginia Secession Convention, just two days after President Lincoln's call for troops to subdue the rebellion. Delegates, contingent upon popular approval, voted to secede from the Union and become part of the Confederacy. Led by John S. Carlile of Clarksburg, many western delegates marched out of the Secession Convention, pledging to frame a state government loyal to the Union.[5] The secession of Virginia unleashed a dramatic life altering debate in the western section of Virginia as counties sent delegates to a convention that met in Wheeling on May 13, 1861. There, young Granville Davisson Hall, a staunch abolitionist whose father had once been indicted by a Harrison County grand jury for subscribing to "subversive" antislavery newspapers, duly recorded complete accounts of both the First and Second Wheeling Conventions. Hall later became the editor of the *Wheeling Intelligencer* and the second Secretary of State of West Virginia.[6]

In the ensuing debate, clearly many citizens from the western counties saw themselves separated geographically and culturally from their eastern Virginian counterparts on the other side of the Blue Ridge and Allegheny Mountains. As delegate Daniel Lamb proclaimed, "We are in fact a different people. Our social habits are different. Our commercial relations are not with eastern Virginia. Every consideration which can be addressed to the wisdom of statesmen would demand a separation at the proper time and in the proper manner."[7] Not surprisingly, as the country rapidly moved to war, many people of western Virginia hastened to declare their loyalty to the Union.

Granville Davisson Hall
West Virginia Regional and History Collection

Attending this initial Wheeling Convention were delegates from twenty-five counties, but disagreement quickly arose about the legitimacy of Virginia's secession since it had not yet been ratified by popular vote. However, on May 23, 1861, a large statewide majority ratified the secession and Virginia officially became part of the Confederacy. Due to vote tampering and destruction of electoral records, an accurate vote tally from what would become present-day West Virginia cannot be determined, but a large majority voted their opposition in the ballot box.[8] Subsequently, on June 11, 1861, at the Second Wheeling Convention, delegates adopted "A Declaration of the People of Virginia" declaring that the Secession Convention had been called without the consent of the people, making its acts void and called for a reorganization of government. On June 20, 1861, the Wheeling Statehood Convention elected Francis Pierpont of Morgantown, a staunch antislavery advocate, Governor of the Restored Government of Virginia. At this point, two governments claimed to be the legal government of Virginia: one loyal to the Union and one to the Confederacy.

On August 6, 1861, the Second Wheeling Convention reconvened, adopting a dismemberment proposal that allowed for the creation of a new state to be called Kanawha. On October 24, 1861, voters of thirty-nine counties in western Virginia approved the creation of this new Unionist state, which a month later was renamed West Virginia. However, the accuracy of these election results has been questioned since Union troops were stationed at many of the polls to discourage Confederate sympathizers from voting.[9] In addition, by this time, eligible voters opposed to separation from Virginia may not have cast votes believing that their loyalty now belonged to Virginia and the Confederacy. By February 1862, the Constitutional Convention included fifty counties as part of the new state of West Virginia.[10]

As the Second Wheeling Convention drafted a new state constitution, two hurdles loomed: firstly, the constitutionality of changing a state's boundaries without the consent of the effected state; and secondly, slavery still existed in what would become West Virginia. Since the Restored Government of Virginia regarded itself as the legitimate government of the state, it granted itself permission to create West Virginia. In fact, President Lincoln also recognized the Restored Government as the legitimate government of Virginia.[11] Furthermore, United States Secretary of the Treasury Salmon P. Chase addressed the constitutionality issue by acknowledging the desire of people in the western section of Virginia to separate from the Old Dominion when he stated that it was "well known that for many years the people of West Virginia have desired separation on good and substantial grounds." He further assured others concerned about the possible precedent setting separation by stating that, "The case of West Virginia will form no evil precedent."[12] By April 1862, voters in the western part of Virginia had approved a constitution that created the state of West Virginia.

However, the newly written constitution did not outlaw slavery. That same year, to his dismay, Granville Parker, a Cabell County delegate to the state's convention, had discovered "the mysterious and over-powering influence the 'peculiar institution' (slavery) had on men otherwise sane and reliable."[13] When the United States Congress addressed the issue of admitting West Virginia to the Union, Massachusetts Senator Charles Sumner demanded an emancipation clause to prevent the addition of another slave state. Indeed, Gordon Battelle, a leading advocate for statehood and a spokesperson for the Wheeling delegates demanding an abolition provision in the new state constitution, warned that Congress would not accept West Virginia without a slave emancipation clause. Furthermore, Battelle argued that slavery's very existence was detrimental to society as a whole. "The injuries which slavery inflicts upon our own people are manifold and obvious. It practically aims to enslave not merely another race, but our own...(it) puts a lock on every man's mouth who will not shout for and swear by the system."[14] Unfortunately, Battelle did not live to see such a clause. He died serving in the Union Army in 1862.

Gordon Battelle
Source: The Rending of Virginia

Similarly, Archibald Campbell, editor of the *Wheeling Daily Intelligencer* and strong supporter of Lincoln in the 1860 election, predicted that West Virginia would not be accepted into the Union without an emancipation clause.[15] At Lincoln's urging, the state convention added a provision in July of that year allowing for the gradual emancipation of slaves. The resulting Willey Amendment was a compromise that allowed, "all children born to slaves after July 4, 1863, would be free, while slaves under the age of ten would be freed at the age of twenty-one and those between ten and twenty-one years of age would gain their freedom at the age of twenty-five."[16] Consequently, on April 20, 1863, when President Lincoln issued a proclamation admitting West Virginia to the Union after a sixty-day waiting period, it became the last slave state to be admitted to the United States.

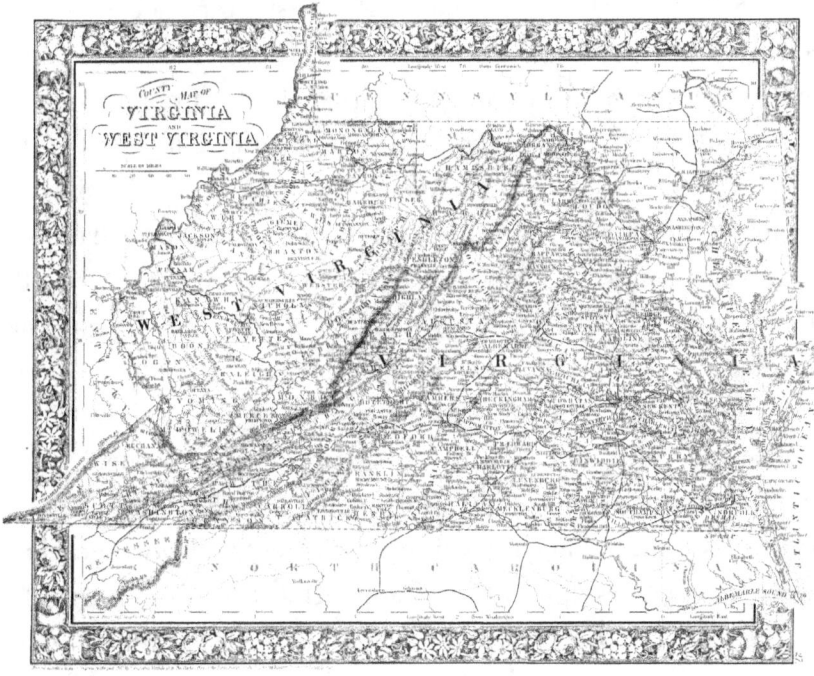

Virginia and West Virginia map, 1863. Library of Congress

However, Frederick Douglass celebrated the Willey Amendment, declaring that "slavery... (had been) stunned nearly to death in West Virginia."[17] The creation of the new state was the only permanent change made to the American map as a result of the Civil War. On June 20, 1863, West Virginia officially became the 35th state admitted to the Union and the new state began to function with the inauguration of Arthur I. Boreman of Parkersburg as the first governor. The following year in its first presidential election, West Virginia voted Republican with 23,152 votes cast for Lincoln while his Democrat opponent General George B. McClellan received 10,438 votes.[18]

Later, in 1865, the state legislature passed an act that immediately abolished slavery before it was required by federal law.[19] Subsequently in March of 1869, West Virginia became the second state to ratify the 15th Amendment, enfranchising African American men by declaring that the "right of citizens of the United States to vote shall not be denied or abridged by the United States, or by any State, on account of race, color, or previous condition of servitude."[20] This ratification occurred six days after Congress proposed it and before it was officially submitted to the states.[21] Although the vote for ratification was perilously close, advocates of the amendment strongly believed in the necessity of citizenship for African American men. State Senator Joseph Thatcher Hoke, representing Berkeley and Jefferson Counties, was highly instrumental in the crucial behind the scenes persuasion of other less than enthusiastic senators. Twenty-five years later, then Judge Hoke presided over the *Williams vs. the Tucker County Board of Education of Fairfax District* case that resulted in an equal school year for both black and white children as well as pay parity for their teachers.

Like Hoke, Senator Waitman T. Willey of Morgantown envisioned a time when there would be no political differences due to race, color or condition of previous servitude.[22] Traveling throughout West Virginia, Senator Willey attempted to spread the message of equality inherent in the 15th Amendment. However, this message often met with armed resistance, particularly among former Confederate West Virginians who found themselves disenfranchised by the dominant Radical Republicans of the Reconstruction era. While over 2,800 African Americans now had the right to vote, an estimated 15,000 to 25,000 white residents remained disenfranchised.[23]

As the editor of the *Wheeling Daily Intelligencer*, Archibald Campbell stated, "Let's bury the hatchet in the ballot box... The enfranchisement of blacks... is... assured... And now as the question of enfranchising the ex-rebels will grow in prominence until some way a solution is reached."[24] Campbell was aided in this pursuit by Granville Davisson Hall who believed that "slavery was a monstrosity – at once a crime and a blunder. The shadow of it fell with the baleful umbrage on the minds of men throughout the republic..."[25] However, seeing the need for healing within the state, Hall advocated the passage of the postwar Flick Amendment that guaranteed the political rights of ex-Confederates and African American men in the newly-formed state.[26]

Once again, West Virginia's internal dilemma mirrored a broader national debate about the ongoing Radical Republican Reconstruction policy. Unable to make his $100,000 bail, Jefferson Davis, former president of the Confederacy, had been held for nearly two years at Fort Monroe in Virginia as he awaited trial for treason against the United States. Surprisingly, among the list of the twenty wealthy men who eventually contributed to posting his bail were some of the staunchest Union proponents. Included in this group were Gerrit Smith, a member of the

"Secret Six" who had funded John Brown's raid on Harper's Ferry, and Cornelius Vanderbilt who had donated his largest steamship to the U.S. Navy.

Most importantly, Horace Greeley, publisher of the *New York Tribune,* justified his contribution to the bail money by admonishing members of the New York Union League Club. "I arraign you as blockheads who would like to be useful to a great and good cause, but don't know how. Your attempt to base a great, enduring party on the hate and wrath necessarily engendered by a bloody civil war, is as though you should plant a colony on an iceberg which had somehow drifted into a tropical ocean."[27] While Greeley's plea for a healing process that would allow the nation to recover from its wounds without further punishing former Confederates would take many years, his vision was both idealistic and pragmatic.

Subsequently, in 1872, West Virginia revised its constitution to include the Flick Amendment that enfranchised former Confederates and guaranteed the political rights of African American men. Similar to provisions in its earlier constitution, black and white children could not attend the same schools and racial intermarriage was outlawed. However, despite the setbacks of the post Reconstruction period, unlike the southern and former border states of the Civil War period, West Virginia remained the only state in the central Appalachian region that continuously respected the right of the ballot for African Americans.[28] Although slavery was now illegal and African American men had the right to vote, the black population in West Virginia declined. Many slave owners had removed slaves into southern states during the Civil War and the young state as of yet did not provide the economic conditions that would encourage

African American migration to the area. Consequently, by 1870, the black population of West Virginia had declined to approximately 18,000, or less than 5 percent of the total population of 442,000.

However, with the expansion of the railroads and the increased industrial demand for coal and timber, West Virginia soon presented genuine economic and political opportunities for African Americans. George H. Edmunds, a prominent black United Mine Workers of America organizer, aptly described African American migration to West Virginia as workers "seeking a man's chance in the world; a chance to... exercise the right of the ballot... (they were) looking for true American citizenship."[29] And as Mother Jones, the "Miners' Angel," and other organizers for the UMWA soon realized, "black miners held the key to the union's future in that state (West Virginia). It wasn't just a matter of whether whites would ever accept 'colored men' as brothers; it was also a question of whether individualistic mountaineers would emulate the black miners by practicing the virtues of solidarity."[30] That hope of shared solidarity was woven into the process of unionization. In effect, the coal mines of West Virginia became the conduit for greater participation in American democracy and improved economic prospects for African Americans.

The new state's motto, Montani Semper Liberi, or Mountaineers Are Always Free, suggests the possibilities that freedom holds for all: native Mountaineers, newcomers from other states, including African Americans, and recent immigrants from southern and eastern Europe, all proudly calling West Virginia their home. Together, this vital burgeoning population of the Mountain State helped to provide the vast natural resources that built industrial America. Despite the long hours, strenuous labor and often hazardous conditions, West Virginia beckoned with the hope of a better life, a life that offered equal opportunities for all.

This is the American dream that Carrie Williams sought for her own children as well as for each child in her classroom in the Coketon Colored School. While this is Carrie's story, it is also the tale of the many hard working, determined, courageous people who settled and farmed the land, who worked in the coal mines and the timberlands, who built and ran the railroads, and who manned the stores and offices in the towns of the Mountain State.

1. "The J.R. Clifford Project, A New Home for Liberty" Brochure, www.jrclifford.org/.
2. Engle, Stephen D. "Mountaineer Reconstruction: Blacks in the Political Reconstruction of West Virginia." *The Journal of Negro History*, vol. 78, no. 3, 1993, pp.139-140.
3. Rice, Connie Park. "'For Men and Measures: The Life and Legacy of Civil Rights Pioneer J.R. Clifford." *Eberly College of Arts and Sciences at West Virginia University*, 2007. p. 5.
4. Dickinson, Jack L. "Confederate Soldiers in West Virginia." www.wvencyclopedia.org/articles/1499.
5. "West Virginia Statehood." *West Virginia Archives & History*, www.wvculture.org/history//statehood.html.
6. Steelhammer, Rick. "Play Tells Story of West Virginia's Statehood." *Charleston Gazette-Mail*, Associated Press,

31 Mar. 2011, www.wvgazettemail.com/ap/ApTopStories/201103310363.
7. Pepper, Charles M. *The Life and Times of Henry Gassaway Davis.* New York, NY, The Century Co., 1920. p. 36.
8. "West Virginia Statehood." *West Virginia Archives & History*, www.wvculture.org/history//statehood.html.
9. Ibid.
10. Ibid.
11. Ibid.
12. Engle, Stephen D. "Mountaineer Reconstruction: Blacks in the Political Reconstruction of West Virginia." *The Journal of Negro History*, vol. 78, no. 3, 1993, p. 137.
13. Ibid., p. 140.
14. "The J.R. Clifford Project" Poster, www.jrclifford.org/.
15. Ibid.
16. "West Virginia Statehood." *West Virginia Archives & History*, www.wvculture.org/history///statehood.html.
17. Engle, Stephen D. "Mountaineer Reconstruction: Blacks in the Political Reconstruction of West Virginia." *The Journal of Negro History*, vol. 78, no. 3, 1993, p. 137.
18. "A West Virginia Timeline." jeff560.tripod.com/wv-hist.html. p.14.
19. Engle, Stephen D. "Mountaineer Reconstruction: Blacks in the Political Reconstruction of West Virginia." *The Journal of Negro History*, vol. 8, no. 3, 1993, p. 140.
20. "The United States Constitution - The U.S. Constitution Online." USConstitution.net, usconstitution.net/const.html.

21. Rice, Connie Park. "'For Men and Measures: The Life and Legacy of Civil Rights Pioneer J.R. Clifford." *Eberly College of Arts and Sciences at West Virginia University*, 2007. p. 35.
22. Engle, Stephen D. "Mountaineer Reconstruction: Blacks in the Political Reconstruction of West Virginia." *The Journal of Negro History*, vol. 78, no. 3, 1993, p. 148.
23. "A Brief History of African Americans in West Virginia." *West Virginia Archives & History*, www.wvculture.org/history/africanamericans/blacks.html.
24. Engle, Stephen D. "Mountaineer Reconstruction: Blacks in the Political Reconstruction of West Virginia." *The Journal of Negro History*, vol. 78, no. 3, 1993, p. 147.
25. "The J.R. Clifford Project" Brochure, www.jrclifford.org/.
26. Ibid.
27. Frail, T. A. "The Trial of the Century That Wasn't ." *Smithsonian Magazine*, vol. 48, no. 2, May 2017, p. 18.
28. Lewis, Ronald L. "From Peasant to Proletarian: The Migration of Southern Blacks to the Central Appalachian Coalfields." *The Journal of Southern History*, vol. 55, no. 1, Feb. 1989, p. 82.
29. Ibid.
30. Green, James R. *The Devil Is Here in These Hills: West Virginia's Coal Miners and Their Battle for Freedom.* New York, NY, Grove Press, 2015. p. 48.

CHAPTER TWO
The Grand Old Man of West Virginia

Henry Gassaway Davis, known in the early twentieth century as West Virginia's "Grand Old Man," is the epitome of the entrepreneur and party boss of the post Civil War period. Like many of his counterparts in this era, Davis was a self-made man. Indeed, it was his vision that propelled the newly created state of West Virginia into its role as the crucial supplier of essential timber and coal to the young nation on the brink of the burgeoning industrial era. Davis created a far-reaching corporate empire based upon his coal and coke interests that coupled with his extensive railroad holdings made him one of the richest and most powerful men in 19th century America. As the principal leader of Davis Coal and Coke Company and the West Virginia Central & Pittsburg Railroad, Davis wielded an enormous impact on the lives of the men and women who lived and worked in his coal and railroad dependent towns. When Carrie Williams filed her suit against the Tucker County Board of Education of Fairfax District, in reality, she was challenging the corporate power that was Henry Gassaway Davis.

Just as the history of West Virginia mirrors national developments, the life of Henry Gassaway Davis correlates with critical moments in American history. Born in Baltimore, Maryland in 1823, Davis was at the center of life and politics in the fledgling state of West Virginia until his death in 1916. The way in which Davis seized opportunities, and through hard work and unrelenting determination, achieved success is a genuine American narrative worthy of acclaim in Ben Franklin's *Poor Richard's Almanac*. His intuitive understanding of the pivotal role that timber, coal and the railroad would play in American national development emerged from his initial viewing of the vast mountainous landscape of what would become West Virginia. This vision played a vital role in catapulting the United States into the modern industrial era and establishing the young nation as a critical force in the international market place.

Davis' family background dates from the Revolutionary War period. His father Caleb was of Welsh ancestry while his mother Louisa was of Irish-Scotch lineage. Caleb had been a soldier in the War of 1812, but in peacetime owned a grocery and feed store in Baltimore. However, Caleb understood that American commerce was changing and the integral role that transportation, particularly railroads such as the B & O, would play in the coming years. As Davis biographer Charles Pepper underscores, "The Baltimore and Ohio Company was the first chartered and fully organized company in the United States for the construction of an extended line of railroad. It was a distinctly Baltimore enterprise. Its early difficulties and the resourcefulness of the men who projected and carried it through... are part of the history of the development of the country through transportation enterprise."[1] When Caleb took his family to see the laying of the cornerstone of what would become the historic Camden Station of the Baltimore and Ohio Railway at the southwest line of the city, he could not foresee the role that this railroad would play in his son's life. Held atop his father's shoulder during the ceremony, five-year-old Henry Gassaway clearly remembered this event and spoke of it fondly in his later years.[2]

Anticipating the railroad's expansion, Caleb moved his family back to their small farm near Woodstock in Howard County, Maryland. Here, he entered into contracts to grade sections of the rail line for the B & O. However, as the aftermath of the Panic of 1837 spread, Caleb, like many of his fellow investors, suffered severe financial setbacks. The family farm and most of their possessions were sold to meet the family's debts.[3] After Caleb's subsequent death, Louisa attempted to maintain the household, but Henry, now a boy in his teens, was thrust into the role of primary economic provider for the family. Former Governor Howard of Maryland assisted the family by giving them a home on his property and paying fifteen-year-old Henry twenty-five cents per day as a farm steward. At this point, Davis' formal education that consisted of attending three-month winter school terms came to an official end. Insisting that his younger brothers stay in school, for the next four years, only his mother assisted young Henry in his education.[4]

However, Henry Gassaway Davis' life took a dramatic turn when Dr. Woodside, a family friend and superintendent of the new railroad extension of the Baltimore and Ohio Railway to Cumberland, Maryland, offered him a position as a freight brakeman at $25 per month.[5] From this vantage, nineteen-year old Davis saw the vast natural resources of what would become West Virginia and, at the same time, developed a heightened appreciation of the role that the railroad would play in the nation's expansion and commercial future. As West Virginia historian Donald Rice attests, "the railroad had more to contribute to the transformation of a rural society to a vibrant economy extracted from the forest, fields, and mines...than any other event."[6] Instinctively understanding this, at a young age Davis had discovered his life's work, quickly earning the nickname, "the energetic brakeman," and promotion to freight conductor and later passenger conductor.

It was in his capacity as passenger conductor that Davis first met Senator Henry Clay, the Great Commoner, who travelled on his train from Cumberland to Washington, D.C. This was the beginning of a life-long friendship, one that fueled Davis' interest in politics and concerns about the conflicts brewing within the United States.[7] As Davis biographer Charles Pepper assessed, "The magnetism of the Great Commoner cast its spell over the train conductor, who became one of his earnest political supporters."[8] This friendship was one of the great factors shaping the future career of Davis; his conversations with Clay became the consummate seminar in the great national issues of the day.[9] Indeed, Davis' first vote for president was cast for the Whig Presidential Candidate Henry Clay in the election of 1844. At this point in his life, Davis could not have foreseen that, like his mentor, much of his public life would be spent in the United States Senate.

In fact, a young Davis was in the crowded Senate Chamber when Henry Clay, John Calhoun and Daniel Webster participated in the great debate that resulted in Clay's Compromise of 1850.[10] The issues at stake were high: what to do with the land acquired in the Mexican Cession as a result of the Mexican American War? Should this territory be opened or closed to slavery? While the Treaty of Guadalupe Hidalgo, ratified in March of 1848, officially ended the conflict, the seething Pandora's Box of sectional conflicts regarding the expansion of slavery was once again opened with such force that for two years Congress remained deadlocked in the controversy.

Due to the Gold Rush of 1849, California had the requisite population for statehood and had already applied for admission to the United States as a free state. An extension of the Missouri Compromise Line of 1820 would have divided California into a half free/half slave state when California's constitution called for the exclusion of slavery. At the same time, the territory of New Mexico governed by army officers sought status as an organized territory with a proposed constitution that also outlawed slavery. For nearly two years, Congress struggled with these issues.

The Compromise of 1850, in effect, nullified the Missouri Compromise of 1820, an earlier achievement of Clay's that had preserved the Union in the on-going debate over slavery. At that time, in order to maintain the balance of free and slave states, the Missouri Compromise admitted Missouri as a slave state and Maine as a free state. In addition, it divided the remaining territory acquired in the Louisiana Purchase along the line 36° 30' north latitude. North of this line, excluding Missouri, "slavery was forever forbidden."[11] Now seventy-three years old and nearing the end of his long career, Clay once again sought a way to maintain unity in the country. Among its prominent provisions, the Compromise of 1850 allowed California to enter the Union as a free state and applied the principle of popular sovereignty to the newly created territories of New Mexico and Utah. It also further strengthened the Fugitive Slave Law, a provision that cost Senator Daniel Webster much support in New England. As a witness to this great debate that shaped the prewar years, Davis saw politics in action in a way that must have impacted and molded his vision of America as well as heightened his understanding of the essential role that a senator may play in this process.

After his appointment as Division Superintendent or General Manager of the line at a salary of $100 per month,[12] Davis was the first railroad executive to institute nighttime runs, a practice that was soon copied by other railroad lines. Davis then became the Piedmont, Virginia agent for the B & O, the most senior position on the line west of Baltimore. Marrying Katherine Bantz in Frederick County, Maryland in 1853, the couple eventually made Piedmont their home. Although this town was in the heart of bituminous coal country, it barely boasted eight to ten primitive houses. In fact, Davis lived in a boxcar for a year while he built a house for his bride who remained in Frederick.[13] Despite its meager beginnings, in Davis' eyes, Piedmont was the gateway to the natural resources that would become the basis of his commercial empire.[14]

However, after only a brief time in his position as the Piedmont agent, Davis resigned in 1858 to devote his time exclusively to his own mercantile lumber and coal interests. Much of Davis' savings from his work on the B & O Railroad and his wife Katherine's inheritance after her father's death had been spent in buying hundreds of acres of land near the Cheat River and its tributaries for as little as fifty to seventy-five cents to a dollar and a half per acre.[15] Including his brother Thomas and later his brother William in his business ventures, he formed H. G. Davis & Company which rapidly built up a thriving trade and was among the first companies to open sawmills in the wilderness operated by men in its pioneer lumber camps.

Henry Gassaway Davis
Library of Congress

In 1858, H. G. Davis & Company, as the principal business concern in the upper Potomac region, created a much needed bank. Incorporated under the Virginia code, the Piedmont Savings Bank in Hampshire County served the needs of the pioneer population of the area. Davis was president of the bank and both of his brothers served as directors.[16] During the Civil War, this section of West Virginia was also a borderland between Union and Confederate troops. H. G. Davis & Company suffered severe losses when Confederate forces raiding Piedmont destroyed thousands of dollars worth of its property.[17] Indeed, Romney in Hampshire County was held fifty-six times by both Union and Confederate forces. Due to the importance of the Baltimore and Ohio Railroad, nearby Keyser exchanged hands fourteen times during the War. When West Virginia became a state, contention developed between Piedmont and New Creek Station (later, Keyser, West Virginia) over the location of the county seat in the newly created Mineral County. However, this dispute was effectively settled in 1867 when the Davis brothers donated land in Keyser for the county courthouse. Despite heavy losses, given his established businesses, Davis was able to enter into highly profitable contracts supplying the Union cause during the war.

However, not actually fighting in the Union Army deeply troubled the forty-year old Davis. When former president of the B & O Railroad Thomas Swann, charged with the responsibility of maintaining the line in operation during the war, heard of Davis' plan to enlist, he quickly took him to the White House to meet with President Lincoln. At six feet tall, Davis considered himself a big man. "But... when Lincoln... came over and, placing both hands on his shoulders, looked down on him... he felt... he wasn't so big a man after all... (when Lincoln said,) Young man... so you want to carry a musket? Isn't it better to carry five thousand muskets? Swann says you are worth that many where you are now. I want you to stay there."[18] Davis returned to his post and continued his work supplying the Baltimore and Ohio Railroad Company with ties and other desperately needed equipment.

After the Civil War ended, H. G. Davis & Company continued to supply the B & O Railroad with timber and coal to repair the extensive damage suffered during the conflict. The former B & O brakeman was now reaping thousands from the road for which he had previously worked for the meager sum of twenty-five dollars per month.[19] Although suffering heavy losses during the Civil War, H. G. Davis & Company had accumulated substantial capital that was then invested in buying several more thousands of acres of timberlands in the Cheat River area in Garret County, Maryland at the summit of the Allegheny Mountains as well as land in Mineral, Grant, Tucker, Preston and Randolph Counties in West Virginia. Much of this land had once been part of the six million acre estate of Thomas, Sixth Lord Fairfax. Few men had the courage to invest so much in this timberland area, let alone to understand the possibilities that coal in the region could bring. In fact, Davis' youngest brother William refused to invest even a dollar in this venture.[20]

A further complicating factor in developing the natural resources of West Virginia was a lack of capital for investment, consequently making the area ripe for outside investors. As historian James Green aptly assesses, "At the end of the Civil War, even the wealthiest landowners and merchants in the new state lacked the access to capital, railroad connections, and land titles they needed to exploit the fabulous wealth of coal reserves... These men yielded to entrepreneurs from the north and the east who would furnish the capital and credit required to build the railroads that would link West Virginia to national markets and open its natural resources to exploitation by industrialists."[21]

Here Henry Gassaway Davis presented a dramatic contrast to most of his fellow West Virginians. Not only did he appreciate the vast coal deposits waiting beneath the rugged terrain, but Davis also possessed the fearless determination to find the capital to combine the mining of coal with the building of a railroad system linking the Allegheny Mountains with the eastern and midwestern markets. According to the West Virginia Institute for the History of Technology and Industrial Archaeology, "Despite early transportation, no serious competitors barked at the heels of Henry Gassaway Davis in the early 1880s when he created his railway-based Upper Potomac coal empire. As *Black Diamond* magazine asserted, without Davis, 'development would have come ultimately, but it would not have progressed to the extent he made possible.' "[22] As Davis acquired each acre and planned each railroad tie, he methodically established an extensive empire that he controlled in the Mountain State. Profits from these investments ultimately made Henry Gassaway Davis the consummate millionaire.

A keystone of Davis' vision was the creation of the Potomac and Piedmont Coal and Railway Company that ultimately developed into the West Virginia Central & Pittsburg Railway. In 1866 during his tenure in the West Virginia House of Delegates, Davis had secured a charter for this company, granting him the right to construct railroad lines in Mineral, Grant, Tucker and Randolph Counties. This charter further accorded him vast powers to develop natural resources in north-central West Virginia. Davis strategically planned railway routes around future coal and timber sites. Particularly in the northern counties of the state, dense timberlands were a formidable wilderness, making an estimate of the underlying coal deposits nearly impossible. However, Davis had made multiple excursions into this sparsely populated area where he noted the types of timber available and the location of coal deposits. Using this vital information, Davis then projected the most efficient railroad routes he was to build.[23]

Clearly, Davis was embarked upon a journey that would catapult him into leadership in his young state. As West Virginia struggled to establish itself in the post Civil War period, he entered state politics as a Union-Conservative Party member. Two fundamental concerns confronted the young state: political issues arising from the recent conflict; and administrative policies regarding taxes, finances, industrial development and internal improvements.[24] Although a strong Union man during the Civil War, Davis sought reconciliation with the former Confederate supporters in his state and staunchly opposed the loyalty oaths that the Radical Republicans sought to require of fellow West Virginians. Advocating the "Let Up" policy, Davis sought to move away from the divisiveness of radical politics towards ex-Confederates. At the same time, he believed that granting suffrage to African American men was "a grave mistake," a stance that solidified his position with many of his constituents.[25] Despite this opposition, West Virginia was among the first states to ratify the 15th Amendment. Eventually, these issues were resolved in 1871 by the state legislature's passage of the Flick Amendment to the state constitution granting suffrage to all male citizens regardless of race or participation in the Confederate cause.

Davis became a lifelong Democrat after political trickery by Republican opponents cost him an election to the state legislature. Disgusted by this dishonesty, Davis joined the opposition.[26] In 1865, he was elected to the lower branch of the state legislature as a Democrat and two years later to the state senate. His tenure in government contributed to the necessary financial and taxation codification for the young state. As a state legislator, Davis also helped to create a public school system and changed the Agricultural College of West Virginia at Morgantown to West Virginia University. Of eminent importance to him was the improvement of roads and internal navigational systems within the state.

As a delegate to the Democratic National Convention in New York City in 1868, Davis interacted with representatives from the entire country. Despite his party affiliation, his political views, especially those regarding the importance of a protective tariff and the burgeoning industrial direction of the nation during the post Civil War period, reflected the values of the new Republican Party. With the Compromise of 1877, Radical Reconstruction ended and the era of the pro big business Republican Party was born. However, Davis remained a staunch Democrat, but clearly one who understood the relationship of industry, business and finance and the role that government, both federal and state, played in this triumvirate. These factors coalesced into the powerful role that Davis came to perform in both the national forum and the economic development of West Virginia.

In 1870, a hotly contested race for reelection against the Republican W.H.H. Flick, one of the state's leading Republican politicians, cast the victorious Davis into the role of leader of the Democratic Party in West Virginia. Under his leadership, the young state was loyally Democratic for the next twenty-five years. In 1871, at age forty-eight, Davis was unanimously elected to the United States Senate, a seat that he held until 1883. During his lifetime, he was a delegate to nine Democratic National Conventions and at age eighty was the reluctant Democratic nominee for vice president in 1904, in part because of his ability to bring critically needed funds to the campaign against the Republican incumbent candidate, President Theodore Roosevelt.

As a senator, Davis did not seek the oratorical limelight as many of his contemporaries did; rather his real abilities shone in the committee work of the United States Senate. Here, "his becoming modesty and his desire for doing unostentatious work" made him a power in committee rooms.[27] Known for his mastery of facts and statistics, he became a key figure on the Appropriations Committee, which he eventually chaired for two years. During his senate career, Davis was also a prominent advocate for the creation of a national Department of Agriculture.[28] Similar to his work in the West Virginia state legislature, he promoted federal legislation to develop West Virginia's natural resources by securing substantial appropriations for improvement of the state's waterways and the system of dams and locks in the Great Kanawha, Monongahela and other rivers.

Understanding the essential role of the railroad in creating a national market place, his most important work was done on the old Transportation Committee, which eventually created the Interstate Commerce Commission.[29] Although reticent that Congress could exercise power to regulate commerce among the states, Davis served on the Senate Select Committee hearing testimony regarding the need for regulation of interstate commerce. In 1887, the Interstate Commerce Act was eventually enacted, years after Davis had left the United States Senate.

Davis found himself in the role of the party boss that evolved after the assassination of President James A. Garfield by Charles Guiteau, a distraught office seeker. The new president, Chester A. Arthur, himself a long time beneficiary of the old patronage system which culminated in his appointment as Collector of the Port of New York Custom House and later position as Vice President, advocated civil service reform. When the Civil Service Reform Act became law in 1883, a new party boss emerged. Gone was the old patronage system that had rested upon "three principles: appointment for political considerations, congressional control of appointments, and rotation of office holders. The system stressed personal loyalty and the 'spoils' of victory."[30] The new party boss worked closely with lobbyists of utilities, railroads, industries, and manufacturers. Henry G. Davis and his son-in-law Stephen B. Elkins ran respectively the Democratic and Republican parties of West Virginia.[31] For Davis, his understanding of the relationship of the coal and timber industries to not only the railroads, but also to the development of a national marketplace clearly impacted his role as both senator and party boss.

However, the Grand Old Man of West Virginia was not totally wedded to the party politics of his era. Unlike many of his party, Davis was a "Protection Democrat" who did not believe in unlimited free trade.[32] In fact, he gave 1888 Republican Presidential Candidate Benjamin Harrison his tacit support. Davis also helped his Republican son-in-law Stephen B. Elkins win a senate seat where he influenced tariff legislation beneficial to the Davis-Elkins business interests.

Davis chose not to run for the senate in 1883 in order to devote himself to his coal, timber, banking and railroad interests in his home state where he had already solidified these commercial enterprises into an empire. His education in the United States Senate only reinforced what he had learned years ago in the West Virginia state legislature: the intertwined nature of business, finance and government was the underpinning of economic success in the post Civil War period. Furthermore, his tenure in the U.S. Senate had cast him into contact with the leading financiers and politicians of the nation. Highly respected for his business acumen, Davis had little difficulty in finding investors eager to join in his plan to span what was described as "the almost unsurmountable Alleghanies" with the West Virginia Central and Pittsburg Railway.[33]

Financial supporters of this project abound in the roll call of the United States Senate. Known as the statesmen's railroad, investors included Senators James Blaine of Maine, Stephen B. Elkins of West Virginia, Arthur Gorman (Davis' cousin on his mother's side) and William Pinkney Whyte, both of Maryland, William Windom of Wisconsin, and Thomas Bayard of Delaware.[34] Another prominent investor was Richard C. Kerens of Missouri, the American ambassador to Austria-Hungary from 1909 -1913. Kerens also built a country estate near Elkins.[35] Many towns along the railway route bear their names and all remained associated with the WVC&P until it was sold in 1902.

When Davis built the West Virginia Central & Pittsburg Railroad, he used the same 1866 charter that he had received from the state government to build the Potomac and Piedmont

Coal and Railway Company. Work officially commenced in 1880 and by November 1884, track stretched from Cumberland, Maryland to the Davis family namesake community in Tucker County, West Virginia. This in itself was a major accomplishment given the rugged terrain of the region. "A large part of Tucker County was absolutely a primeval wilderness. The flat top of the mountain at an elevation of 3,000 feet was covered by almost impenetrable forests... There were no trails."[36] Located a few miles away from the Davis owned coal and coke producing area in Thomas named for his brother, the town of Davis, incorporated in 1889, boasted a population of 909 that in ten years grew to 2,319.[37] The town also became the site of the first bank in Tucker County, the National Bank of Davis, an essential commercial component in the fast developing area. Thomas Beall Davis was the first president with Henry Gassaway Davis among the directors.

In 1888 when Davis extended the WVC&P to Hendricks just ten miles south of Thomas, he encountered dramatic geological impediments as he expanded his railroad line through the rugged terrain of the Blackwater Canyon. "One year and ten miles later, the Black Fork grade... was completed. This was an astonishing feat considering that along the way cuts sometimes hundreds of feet high were made into Backbone Mountain in order to facilitate construction. Other obstacles encountered were deep ravines and several rushing tributary streams... trestles were often built to keep construction moving, with workers returning later to place fill and remove trestles and build gigantic stone archways... all work was done by hand. It was considered at the time to be nearly an impossible task."[38] Added to the complexity of this building is the Black Fork's steep gradient averaging 2.34 percent, at times more than 3 percent, as it climbs 1,236 feet over its ten-mile course.[39]

Eventually, Davis extended the WVC&P to Elkins, West Virginia, the seat of Randolph County and home of his palatial estate, Graceland. The November 1889 arrival of the railroad produced immediate economic benefits for the town and county. Coal production doubled relatively quickly and eventually quadrupled before leveling off to an annual production of three million tons from mines in the area.[40] The timber industry also increased as lumber production could be more easily moved by the main line railroad and the interconnecting logging railroads carrying lumber to mills for processing.[41] Remaining as president until 1902, Davis sold the West Virginia Central & Pittsburg to the Gould financial interests where it became part of the Western Maryland Railway Company.

Indeed, the West Virginia Central & Pittsburg Railway had unlocked the vast resources of the Mountain State. As Davis pushed the railroad line through Tucker, Barbour, Randolph and Pocahontas Counties of West Virginia and connected it with the Baltimore & Ohio Railroad in Cumberland, Maryland, he achieved the means of transporting his coal and lumber to eastern markets. "West Virginia's hidden wealth... the opening of vast coal mines... the hewing a way through the virgin forests and the erection of gigantic sawmills" became accessible to the young industrial nation by Davis' extensive railroad construction.[42] Now, the "energetic brakeman" was poised to become one of the most powerful and influential entrepreneurs in the newly defined international marketplace.

When Henry Gassaway Davis formed Davis Coal and Coke Company in partnership with his brothers and his son-in-law,

Senator Stephen B. Elkins, he launched a corporate empire that supplied the ever increasing demand for timber, coal and coke, all transported by his own railroad system to a rapidly developing industrial nation and beyond. Davis centered his far-reaching corporate endeavors in Tucker County's Fairfax District, consisting of six towns: Thomas, Pierce, Benbush, Douglas, Coketon and William with a total population of approximately 5,000. Here, Davis owned over 135,000 acres of coal rich land and employed 2,500 men of eighteen different nationalities. In fact, in 1903, Davis Coal and Coke Company hired Wladyslaw Dackiewicz, fluent in eight languages, as a much needed interpreter.[43] In 1883, the company had coal ready for shipment when the West Virginia Central and Pittsburg Railroad reached Davis, West Virginia, one year later. Davis Coal and Coke Company quickly ranked among the largest and most widely known coal companies in the world.[44]

As early as 1887, the company had constructed two experimental coke ovens to test the quality of the coal, and by 1897, 370 coke ovens were in operation. Coke was in high demand in making steel and iron, and due to the WV&P, Davis had a ready means of transporting his product to steel producing areas such as Pittsburgh.[45] Soon, the one-and-one half mile stretch between Thomas and Douglas was aglow with fires of over 1,000 coke ovens.[46] In addition, the company operated two power plants and worked nine coal mines within one mile of their central office at Coketon in Tucker County. During its existence, Davis Coal and Coke averaged a yearly production of 1.5 million tons of coal from its mines.[47]

Always remaining a railroad man, Davis later built the Coal & Iron Railroad extending from Elkins to Durbin and the Coal &

Coke Railroad from Elkins that reached Charleston in 1906. In particular, the Coal & Coke, financed completely by Davis' own funds, made the West Virginia counties of Upshur, Lewis, Braxton, Gilmer, Clay and Kanawha accessible for development.[48] In building this railroad, eighty-year old Davis took his secretary and a group of engineers along two hundred and fifty miles of rugged country on horseback where he "initiated the other members of the party into the mysteries of camp life, and took his morning bath before sunrise, in the icy waters of the mountain streams."[49]

Although no longer a senator, Davis remained active in national life. In addition to his role as a delegate to multiple Democratic National Conventions and as a vice presidential nominee in 1904, Davis was appointed by three presidents as the American representative to successive Pan-American Conferences from 1889 to 1902. His belief in the importance of an intercontinental railroad to connect North and South America in a thriving trade venture reminiscent of his former mentor Henry Clay's enhanced American System led him to become the chairman of the Pan-American Railroad Committee for several years.

Within West Virginia, Davis continued his public service. In 1901, Governor Albert B. White appointed him to the State Commission responsible for revising the West Virginia tax laws, a code that he had helped to create during his original tenure in the newly created state legislature. His last public service was chairman of the Semi-Centennial Commission in 1913 where he helped to plan West Virginia's "Golden Jubilee" celebrating fifty years of statehood.

Like many of his counterparts, Davis adhered to Andrew Carnegie's belief system presented in *The Gospel of Wealth*, which advocated that the wealthy share their surplus in a manner that would most broadly benefit society. Known for his philanthropic works, Davis, along with his son-in-law Senator Stephen B. Elkins, founded Davis and Elkins College in his adopted hometown of Elkins. His other humanitarian endowments include Davis Memorial Hospital, the Davis Memorial Presbyterian Church, the establishment of several YMCAs, the Davis Free School in Piedmont and the Charleston Child Shelter.

For the elder Davis, "Life has been full of toil, but his spirit is as buoyant, his interest in affairs as keen, and his activity as driving as when he first twisted a brake on the Baltimore and Ohio Railroad."[50] Davis died in Washington, D.C., on March 11, 1916, at age ninety-three. Perhaps a fitting epitaph to his life, a life that spanned nearly a century of the nation's history, are his own words to a reporter for the Baltimore and Ohio Railway Magazine for Employees. "America is the paradise of democracy. Every young man down there in the mines, in the offices of the railroad, in the machine shops and in the stores, has a hundred opportunities where I had one."[51] How Davis seized this opportunity as a nineteen-year old brakeman for the B & O Railroad is intertwined in the history of West Virginia and that of a young nation on its way to world power.

1. Pepper, Charles M. *The Life and Times of Henry Gassaway Davis.* New York, NY, The Century Co., 1920. p. 9.
2. Ibid., p. 10.
3. Ibid., p. 13.
4. "Death of Henry Gassaway Davis." *West Virginia Archives & History,* www.wvculture.org/history/government/davishenry02.html.
5. Ibid.
6. Rice, Donald L. *Randolph 200: A Bicentennial History of Randolph County, West Virginia: a Pictorial and Documentary Sampler.* Walsworth Publishing Company, 1987. Third Printing, 1999, p. 66.
7. "Death of Henry Gassaway Davis." *West Virginia Archives & History,* www.wvculture.org/history/government/davishenry02.html.
8. Pepper, Charles M. *The Life and Times of Henry Gassaway Davis.* New York, NY, The Century Co., 1920. p. 23.
9. "Remarkable Career of the Late Henry Gassaway Davis." *B and O Magazine,* vol. 3, 1914. p. 38-39.
10. Pepper, Charles M. *The Life and Times of Henry Gassaway Davis.* New York, NY, The Century Co., 1920. p. 22.
11. Blum, John M. *The National Experience: A History of the United States.* 8th ed., San Diego, New York, Chicago, Atlanta, Washington D.C., London, Sydney, and Toronto, Cengage Learning, January 2, 1993. p. 219.
12. Pepper, Charles M. *The Life and Times of Henry Gassaway Davis.* New York, NY, The Century Co., 1920. p. 24.
13. Ibid., p. 27.

14. "Remarkable Career of the Late Henry Gassaway Davis." *B and O Magazine*, vol. 3, 1914. p. 39.
15. "Death of Henry Gassaway Davis." *West Virginia Archives & History*, www.wvculture.org/history/government/davishenry02.html.
16. Pepper, Charles M. *The Life and Times of Henry Gassaway Davis*. New York, NY, The Century Co., 1920. p. 28.
17. Maxwell, Hu. *The History of Randolph County, West Virginia*. Morgantown, WV, The Acme Publishing Company, 1898. p. 364.
18. Pepper, Charles M. *The Life and Times of Henry Gassaway Davis*. New York, NY, The Century Co., 1920. pp. 31-32.
19. "Death of Henry Gassaway Davis." *West Virginia Archives & History*, www.wvculture.org/history/government/davishenry02.html.
20. Pepper, Charles M. *The Life and Times of Henry Gassaway Davis*. New York, NY, The Century Co., 1920. p. 32.
21. Green, James R. *The Devil Is Here in These Hills: West Virginia's Coal Miners and Their Battle for Freedom*. New York, NY, Grove Press, 2015. p. 17.
22. "Coketon and Henry G. Davis" - Excerpt from *A Report of the West Virginia Institute for The History of Technology and Industrial Archaeology*, 1994. 12 Aug. 2006, www.jrclifford.org/images/PioneerPressCentEdition.pdf. p. 4.
23. Pepper, Charles M. *The Life and Times of Henry Gassaway Davis*. New York, NY, The Century Co., 1920. p. 93.
24. Ibid., p. 37.

25. Ibid., p. 44.
26. "Remarkable Career of the Late Henry Gassaway Davis." *B and O Magazine*, vol. 3, 1914. p. 40.
27. "Death of Henry Gassaway Davis." *West Virginia Archives & History*, www.wvculture.org/history/government/davishenry02.html.
28. Ibid.
29. "Remarkable Career of the Late Henry Gassaway Davis." *B and O Magazine*, vol. 3, 1914. p. 41.
30. Blum, John M. *The National Experience: A History of the United States.* 6th ed., San Diego, New York, Chicago, Atlanta, Washington D.C., London, Sydney, and Toronto, Harcourt College Publishers, January 28, 1985. p. 502.
31. Ibid.
32. "Remarkable Career of the Late Henry Gassaway Davis." *B and O Magazine*, vol. 3, 1914. p. 40.
33. "Death of Henry Gassaway Davis." *West Virginia Archives & History*, www.wvculture.org/history/government/davishenry02.html.
34. Doyle, James T. "Brakeman—Builder—Benefactor A Tribute to Henry Gassaway Davis, Who Began His Business Career on the Baltimore and Ohio." *B and O Magazine*, vol. 3, 1914. p. 47.
35. "West Virginia Division of Culture and History." *National Register of Historic Places - United States Department of Interior*, www.wvculture.org/shpo/nr/pdf.
36. Pepper, Charles M. *The Life and Times of Henry Gassaway Davis.* New York, NY, The Century Co., 1920. p. 100.

37. Phillips, Cynthia A. *Images of Tucker County*. Charleston, SC, Arcadia Publishing, 2005. p. 73.
38. Friends of Blackwater. Brochure. *West Virginia Central & Pittsburgh Railroad and Henry Gassaway Davis's Legacy.*
39. Ibid.
40. Rice, Donald L. *Randolph 200: A Bicentennial History of Randolph County, West Virginia: a Pictorial and Documentary Sampler.* Walsworth Publishing Company, 1987. Third Printing, 1999. p. 66.
41. Ibid.
42. Doyle, James T. "Brakeman—Builder—Benefactor A Tribute to Henry Gassaway Davis, Who Began His Business Career on the Baltimore and Ohio." *B and O Magazine*, vol. 3, 1914. p. 46.
43. Phillips, Cynthia A. *Images of Tucker County*. Charleston, SC, Arcadia Publishing, 2005. p. 65.
44. Friends of Blackwater. Brochure *West Virginia Central & Pittsburgh Railroad and Henry Gassaway Davis's Legacy.*
45. Phillips, Cynthia A. *Images of Tucker County*. Charleston, SC, Arcadia Publishing, 2005. p. 60.
46. Friends of Blackwater. Brochure *Walking Tour of Thomas, West Virginia.*
47. Phillips, Cynthia A. *Images of Tucker County*. Charleston, SC, Arcadia Publishing, 2005. p. 60.
48. "Death of Henry Gassaway Davis." *West Virginia Archives & History,* www.wvculture.org/history/government/davishenry02.html.
49. "Remarkable Career of the Late Henry Gassaway Davis."

B and O Magazine, vol. 3, 1914. p. 42.
50. Maxwell, Hu. *The History of Randolph County, West Virginia*. Morgantown, WV, The Acme Publishing Company, 1898. p. 366.
51. "Remarkable Career of the Late Henry Gassaway Davis." *B and O Magazine*, vol. 3, 1914. p. 38.

CHAPTER THREE
The Miners

Life in the West Virginia mining towns created after the American Civil War was a mixture of strenuous labor, difficult living conditions and hazardous working environments. At the same time, miners and their families envisioned a means to a better life for themselves and their children and experienced a real sense of pride in work accomplished. Despite often overwhelming difficulties, they remained hopeful that their belief in the American promise was achievable in the coalfields of West Virginia. Native Mountaineers as well as citizens from other states quickly flocked to the fast growing mining towns. In particular, from 1880 through the early part of the twentieth century, African Americans seeking an alternative to the agrarian impoverishment of sharecropping in the New South now called West Virginia home. Also, employee rosters listed an influx of immigrants, especially from southern and eastern Europe as developing industries in West Virginia beckoned with the promise of a livelihood in their new homeland.

However, while life as a miner offered the hope of an improved life style, according to the West Virginia Archives and History, statistically a United States soldier had a greater chance of surviving a World War I battle than a West Virginian working in the coal mines.[1] To say that life was tenuous as a miner is an understatement, but for the coal miners of West Virginia, the danger of a day's work was at times overwhelming. In 1890, the American Federation of Labor "declared the nation's coal miners in worse shape than any group of wage earners..."[2] Coal miners found an advocate in the social critic Henry Demarest Lloyd who sought to bring attention to the deplorable conditions in which miners worked for little pay. "(The coal diggers) spend ten hours a day in their caverns, pitch dark, except for the flicker and glimmer of the little lamp in the front of his cap... They have to work on their knees, or lying on their side... while digging at the ceiling... This hard work in a room three feet or three feet six inches high, hundreds of feet below the surface, in the gloom of perpetual night... the miner (feeling)... threaten(ed)... daily with death or mutilation; and rewarding his toil with less than the cost of subsistence."[3] Epitomizing these harrowing working conditions, West Virginia led the nation in the number of mine fatalities.

The Mountain State lagged far behind other major coal producing states in regulating mining conditions. The first mine safety acts creating the post of mine inspector as well as providing for drainage and ventilation requirements were not passed until 1883. Despite pleas from the mine inspector, further legislation was not passed until 1897. This act expanded the mining districts to four and created the position of Chief Mine Inspector. In 1905, the West Virginia Department of Mines was finally established.

Six mine disasters occurred that year, the greatest number in any one-year period. Two years later in December of 1907, the nation's worst coal disaster occurred at the Fairmont Coal Company Mine in Monongah, Marion County, West Virginia. Explosions in mines No. 6 and No. 8 killed 361 men and boys leaving over one thousand widows and fatherless children.[4] Yet, mine rescue training did not begin until 1917.[5]

Man with punching machine to drill into coal
Library of Congress

Ironically, the Fairmont mining disaster occurred where the first commercial coal mine was opened in 1818. According to historian James Green, West Virginia was a coal treasure trove. "Few regions in the world were as well-endowed with such carbon deposits, a commonly known fact by 1765."[6] As early as 1770, George Washington had noted "a cole hill on fire" near West

Columbia in Mason County. Thomas Jefferson also commented in *Notes on the State of Virginia* that the land in western Virginia "would yield abundant quantities of the fuel." In the Treaty of Hard Labour three years later, the Cherokees relinquished their claim to land south of the Great Kanawha River, site of the first coal deposits in western Virginia that would eventually be mined by slaves and used as fuel for the salt furnaces of Charleston.[7] Initially, local farmers and slaves surface mined the coal, carrying it away in baskets and sacks for home use. However, with coal deposits existing in fifty-three of the fifty-five counties in what would become West Virginia, extensive mining developed in the mid 1850s.[8] Total coal production reached 300,000 tons by 1840 of which 200,000 tons were used in the Kanawha salt furnaces while the remainder was used in homes and small factories in Wheeling.

Other commercial coal ventures developed in what became West Virginia prior to the Civil War, but it was the 1851 coming of the Baltimore and Ohio Railroad reaching Piedmont, Virginia (later West Virginia), that allowed for coal shipments to Baltimore. When Henry Gassaway Davis became the B & O Railroad agent for Piedmont, he not only assumed the most senior position on the line west of Baltimore, but also first encountered the vast bituminous coal country that became the basis of his corporate empire. By 1853, the B & O stretched as far as Wheeling, opening the area for development of mining interests. However, the outbreak of the Civil War interrupted the burgeoning industry and it would be the later continued expansion of the railroads that would catapult the young state into a leading supplier of coal for the nation. In the post Civil War period, West Virginia's timber and coal industries boomed as railroads spread across the young state. During the 1870s, the Chesapeake & Ohio Railway stretched from Richmond, Virginia to its new terminus on the Ohio River at Huntington named for Collis P. Huntington, the railroad builder who clearly understood the connection between the coal industry and the means to transport the essential product. Later, Henry Gassaway Davis created the West Virginia Central & Pittsburg Railway with its subsequent extensions within the state to transport coal and timber to eastern and midwestern markets.

New mining towns sprouted up along the rail lines and West Virginia experienced a surge in its population. According to the 1870 census, the state population was 442,014, and by 1880 it had grown to 618,457, and to 762,704 by 1890.[9] As newcomers flocked to the state, the population steadily rose from 958,800 in 1900, to 1,221,119 in 1910, and to 1,463,701 by 1920.[10] Many of the newcomers to West Virginia were immigrants from southern and eastern Europe. A common characteristic of the coal mining towns was the multiplicity of languages spoken by the residents, creating a need for companies to engage multilingual personnel. For Davis Coal and Coke Company, as the employer of miners of eighteen different nationalities, Wladyslaw Dackiewicz filled a key position as a translator/interpreter.[11]

Within the United States, many African Americans migrated northward from southern states. In 1860 prior to the Civil War, 21,144 blacks lived in what would become West Virginia. Of that number 2,773 were free and 18,371 were slaves.[12] As the Civil War commenced, many slaveholders sought refuge in Virginia and other southern states. Consequently, by 1870, the African American population declined to approximately 17,980. However, this segment of the population grew to 25,886 by 1880 and rose dramatically to 64,173 by 1910 and reached 114,893 in 1930.[13] Clearly, West Virginia represented a unique opportunity for African Americans seeking an alternative to the agrarian economy of the South where the majority of blacks resided.

As Radical Reconstruction formally ended in the Compromise of 1877 and a vision of the New South came to fruition, the freedmen found themselves with steadily reduced political and economic prospects. While the 14th and 15th Amendments still existed, a succession of Supreme Court decisions gradually eliminated their impact in the South. Furthermore, the Supreme Court voided Charles Sumner's last great endeavor on behalf of African Americans by nullifying the Civil Rights Act of 1875. The primary tools of disenfranchisement were the poll tax, registration laws, and literacy and property qualifications, some with the "understanding clause" or the "grandfather clause" as loopholes to admit poor whites and illiterates. Consequently, black voter turnout dropped an average of 62 percent.[14] The enactment of Jim Crow laws that mandated racial segregation in all public facilities reinforced disenfranchisement by legalizing second-class citizenship. In 1890, Mississippi revised its state constitution in order to further codify this social and political order. Other southern states quickly followed suit. The Republican Party of Radical Reconstruction that had once protected the freedmen had given way to the new Republican Party of big business, banking and the protective tariff.

Coupled with the steady loss of political gains, at the same time, the freedmen found themselves locked into an agrarian economy based upon the twin principles of sharecropping and the lien system. As sharecroppers or tenant farmers, African Americans worked the land once owned by the planters, but now held primarily by merchants and other newcomers to the South. Although the census of 1880 reported a dramatic increase in the number of farms since 1860, in reality, the average farm was less than half its former size. The old plantation system still remained. It had simply morphed into a new model with sharecroppers doing the work of the former slaves. In addition, sharecroppers were dependent on the owner for the tools, work animals and feed necessary for the farming that produced their portion of the crops. As tenant farmers, the landlord/owner kept part of the crop as rent.

Intrinsic to the impoverishment of sharecropping was the lien system where merchants provided the necessary credit for supplies at exorbitant interest rates as high as 60 percent a year. This lien was to be paid off from the sharecropper's already meager portion of the profit from the crops.[15] In rural areas where banks were few, blacks had little choice but to borrow on their crops from merchants only too eager to make an inflated profit on their loan. Added to this bleak agrarian outlook, the skilled crafts work that African Americans had formerly performed on the plantations was now reserved to whites only and the young labor unions soon found ways to freeze out their black counterparts. The promise of forty acres and a mule had long ago evaporated, leaving the freedman in the status of a peon. It is not surprising that African Americans, particularly those a generation or more removed from slavery, sought a better life in the coalfields of West Virginia.

Life in the fast growing mining towns of West Virginia soon became an integral part of an economic system controlled by the coal industry. Unlike small town life across most of America, the West Virginia mining town owed its very existence and livelihood to the dominant coal company of that area. In addition, the town's lifeline was the railroad, a necessary component in delivering the coal product to market. Frequently, mine owners were also shareholders or even sole owners of these railway lines.

Consequently, the location of the mining towns and even their naming was a direct result of the coal company's interconnection with the railroads. For example, Henry Gassaway Davis, the founder of both Davis Coal and Coke Company and the West Virginia Central & Pittsburg Railroad, personally selected town sites and named them for family members and fellow investors. Initially nicknamed Stumptown because a pedestrian could make their way across town by hopping from one stump to another,[16] Davis in West Virginia owes its name to Henry Gassaway Davis who had the thickly forested land cleared for an extension of his West Virginia Central & Pittsburg Railway. Similarly, the nearby town of Thomas, headquarters of Davis Coal & Coke Company, was named for his brother. By 1883, the major rail lines in West Virginia were completed and coal production totaled nearly 3 million tons.[17]

With the development of mining towns came a unique methodology of securing the necessities of life. Since many of these new towns owed their very existence to the coal and railroad interests that built them, mine owners planned the town's arrangement from selecting the location of housing, schools, churches and even merchandise outlets. The power of the mine owner extended into all aspects of life including selecting teachers, ministers and the location of the company store as well as choosing its managerial staff. Davis was true to this model. For example, by 1893 when the Catholic population in Thomas numbered one hundred, H. G. Davis personally selected the

Brown and Third Streets' corner lot that he donated for the new Catholic Church, St. Thomas.[18]

Usually, these company-owned communities were unincorporated towns with no elected officials. Although county sheriffs, commissioners, state representatives and judges could exercise some legal authority over the area, these officials generally respected the coal towns as private property, allowing corporate entities to govern the communities they owned.[19] This is true of the unincorporated company-owned town of Coketon where Carrie Williams sued the Tucker County Board of Education of Fairfax District. In this case, Carrie Williams was, in reality, suing Henry Gassaway Davis, one of the most powerful and influential men in West Virginia and the country as a whole.

Unlike workers in factories in northern cities, miners often lived in company housing. This was especially true in West Virginia where nearly 79 percent of miners and their families lived in company housing as compared to 24 percent of miners in Ohio.[20] However, the relationship was not one of a landlord to a tenant. In West Virginia, the state courts had established the relationship to be "that of a master to a servant... the law allowed the owner to summarily evict families and to inspect miners' houses without a warrant."[21] Women especially were negatively impacted by this arrangement in the event of a husband's death whether it was from natural causes or a mine disaster. On the average, widows and their dependents had to vacate company housing in a short time period, usually two weeks after a miner's death. Since many women were recent immigrants who had left their family support systems in the hope of securing a better life, they were faced with the prospect of remarriage or removal.[22]

In addition, miners were confronted with other economic pitfalls. Before even entering a coal mine, workers had to lease the requisite tools and equipment from the company. These fees, along with the rent, were then deducted from the miner's pay. Coal mine owners also provided company stores that often charged over-inflated prices. An integral part of this economic system was the use of company scrip. Mine owners developed their own monetary system by paying workers in scrip in the form of tokens, currency or credit rather than in dollars. Initially, scrip was offered as a convenience to miners who could shop at the company store without having cash or paying interest on a loan.[23] However, as the use of scrip evolved, it generated resentment among miners because it limited them to shopping in the company store with its frequently inflated prices. Company owners refused to buy back scrip in United States currency, and if miners sold it to traders or merchants, it was usually discounted 25 to 30 percent less than its dollar value.[24] From the owner's perspective, an added benefit of this system was that the coal company did not have to keep a large amount of United States currency in supply.

Another way that miners were denied their proper pay was through the system of cribbing. Generally, workers were paid according to the tons of coal mined. Coal was transported from the mines in cars that usually held two thousand pounds of coal. However, cars were altered to hold more than this amount, but the miners were only paid for the two thousand pounds of coal when the amount might be as much as five hundred pounds greater. Also rock and slate might be mixed in with the coal, causing miners to have money docked from their pay. This was determined by a checkweighman who worked for the company owners. As this practice became increasingly loathsome, the United Mine Workers took over the position of checkweighman in the process of unionization.²⁵

Train-load of ore and miners outside Davis Coal and Coke Company
Library of Congress

Unlike his 1858 business venture in the Upper Potomac region where he had created a critically needed bank for the pioneer population who worked for him, in establishing Davis Coal and Coke Company in Coketon/Thomas, Henry Gassaway Davis followed the economic model that worked so successfully for other coal companies. Prior to its incorporation in 1892, Thomas had a population of 693. By 1920, the town reached its greatest level of 2099. The black population rose from 183 in 1890, to 253 in 1900.²⁶ Most of the African Americans lived in nearby Coketon, the central mining facility and headquarters of the Davis Coal and Coke Company. In the mile and one half stretch along the Northfork of the Blackwater River, one thousand ovens burned two hundred and fifty days a year producing 200,000 tons of coke in 1904 alone. The nearby nine mines shipped over one million tons of coal from 1915 to 1921, making it the sixth most productive operation in West Virginia. D C & C Co. also provided the first paved roads in the area as well as furnishing electricity to the local towns.

Miners and their families lived in the duplex housing structures within easy distance of the mines and coke ovens of Coketon/Thomas. In 1906, four hundred families lived in Davis Coal & Coke Company housing with rent deducted directly from salaries. When compared to other coal company housing, these homes could be described as "adequate." Usually two families lived in each dwelling on a small parcel of land that allowed miners to grow gardens and fruit trees as well as to raise some livestock.[27] Unlike the small towns nestled in the hollows of the Allegheny Mountains, the company town of Coketon and nearby Thomas and Davis sit atop the mountains. In fact, at a lofty 3,100 feet, Davis boasts the highest elevation of any town in the state. In its peak mining days, heavily mixed within the purified mountain air was the coal dust that "peppered people's food, coated their vegetable plants and entered their lungs with every breath they took."[28] Added to this was the noise generated by the tipple's continuous groans as it transported coal to the waiting railroad cars near the one thousand gaseous coke ovens.

In the same manner that company owners planned the public sections of the community, they attempted to structure prevailing societal norms in housing. However, in West Virginia, "...African Americans, Italians and Hungarians never lived more than a few hundred yards 'up the hollow' from native born whites, with whom they worked every day in close proximity and mutual dependency."[29] Miners, white or black, native born or immigrant, lived in similar housing, worked a similar day, and shared the hope and hardship that life in a coal mining town engendered. While the Davis Coal & Coke Company town had "Tony" Row for Italian immigrants and the Coketon Colored School for black children, it also had a shared identity as miners and their families. "Everybody felt a common kinship," one Appalachian miner remembered, "because they all had to work and fare together the same way."[30]

The Davis Coal and Coke Company Store, the Buxton and Landstreet Company incorporated in 1889, opened in 1890 and was located in nearby Coketon away from the other shops in Thomas. This store became the official company store at other Davis Coal & Coke Company mining towns.[31] Here miners and their families used the company trade coins or scrip to purchase various goods from food to clothing to household items. This practice had become so problematic in Maryland that the state outlawed company stores in 1868. Consequently, the Davis Coal and Coke Kempton Mine located in the southwestern corner of Maryland had to locate the Buxton & Landstreet Store across the Potomac River in West Virginia.[32]

A folk song about Henry Gassaway Davis, the railroad owner and the principal shareholder of Davis Coal & Coke Company, paints a harsh portrait. As the song goes, "The men hit for wages, then Henry said, 'what a darn foolish notion you've got in your head! I may run this railroad till the devil goes blind, but I won't raise your wages on the Coal and Coke Line!' "[33] This description of Davis' staunch stand against his railroad workers may be equally applied to his coal miners. Davis based his company interests on the established economic system prevalent in other mining towns. At age eighty, he firmly believed that, "America is the paradise of democracy. Every young man down there in the mines... has a hundred opportunities where I had one."[34] While Davis had seized his opportunity so many years ago, the typical miner working a ten to twelve hour day to pay his rent for company housing, his lease on his company equipment and tools, and his shopping bill at the company store, was left with little means or energy to pursue greater opportunities.

Just as other workers across the country began to unionize, miners formed the United Mine Workers of America in 1890. In addition to seeking the right of collective bargaining, the prohibition of cribbing, alternatives to the company store, and an end to the practice of owners using private guards, miners were also deeply concerned about safety in the mines. When the worst mine disaster in American history occurred at the Fairmont Monongah mines on December 6, 1907, killing approximately 361 men and boys, national attention focused on the coal industry. Weak mine inspection regulation and enforcement resulting in a staggering loss of life catapulted West Virginia's coal mines into prominence as a miner's death trap.

Newspaper reporters on the scene of the disaster at the Fairmont Monongah mines noted that although the coal company did not have an exact record of the number of men in the mines, it did have a precise count of the horses and mules inside at the time of the explosions, contributing to the pervasive miner's lore that the coal companies cared more for mules than men. Compounding the loss of a miner, widows and children had no recourse for economic assistance. Knowing this as a fact of life in the coalfields of West Virginia, miners went to work carrying as many spare coins as they owned in their pockets, knowing that if they died, fellow miners would give these coins to their families.[35]

However, in response to the loss of so many miners, Fairmont Coal Company did provide some compensation to the surviving widows and children. A. Brooks Fleming, former governor of West Virginia and son-in-law of the founder of Fairmont Coal now speaking as a lawyer for the company, declared that while the owners had no legal obligation to help family members of the perished miners, Fairmont Coal would contribute $17,500 to a relief fund for survivors plus an additional small settlement to individual families. At the same time, Fleming was quick to comment, "The Company never for a moment considered it was legally liable... I think that the $2000 distributed among 41 children and 20 widows would be quite a Christmas present."[36] A century later on December 6, 2007, a monument was erected and dedicated by the initiative of the Italian Government to commemorate the loss of so many miners, many of Italian descent. By the end of 1907, the number of mine disasters in West Virginia alone accounted for eight hundred and eighteen deaths. Included in this total were twenty-five miners killed at the Davis Coal and Coke Company mine in Coketon/Thomas.

In 1898, twenty-eight year old John Mitchell became the "boy president" of the United Mine Workers of America. "Intelligent, well spoken and good-looking (some Catholic miners said he looked like a young priest)," Mitchell was admired by union officials for his negotiating skills and by thousands of immigrants who idolized "Johnny d'Mitch."[37] Successfully striking in eastern Pennsylvania, Mitchell forced mine owners to accept the UMWA's terms. Hoping to recruit members in West Virginia, Mitchell sent two experienced UMWA activists, but he knew that he needed "someone who could instill courage and hope in the hearts of the frightened men who mined coal in the Mountain State. The person he hired to play that role would have amazed anyone outside the UMWA's ranks, for he chose a woman old enough to be his grandmother to lead this crucial campaign. Her legal name was Mary Harris Jones, but union men all over industrial America knew her as Mother Jones."[38] As an international organizer, Mother Jones joined the ranks of the UMWA at the salary of $500 a year. Her life's work is a testament to her resiliency, her fierce determination and her commitment to those unfairly treated.

Young Mary Harris was no stranger to hardship. Seeking relief from the Great Hunger, she was a teenager when her family left County Cork, Ireland for Toronto, Canada. Once in Canada, both her immigrant status and her Catholic religion heightened her empathy for people who struggled for acceptance in society. Graduating from the Toronto Normal School in 1859, she moved to Monroe, Michigan, where she briefly taught at a convent school. After relocating to Memphis, Tennessee, she married George Jones, an ironworker and organizer of the National Union of Iron Moulders. Here, her first great tragedy occurred when her husband and four children died in the yellow fever epidemic of 1867. Struggling to rebuild her life, Jones relocated to Chicago where she opened a seamstress business only to have it destroyed in the Great Chicago Fire of 1871.

It was in Chicago that she became involved in union activity, first in the Knights of Labor, where she fought for the striking American Railway Union members in the Pullman Strike, and then in the United Mine Workers of America. Mother Jones had truly found her voice, a voice still sprinkled with an Irish brogue that now resonated with the heartfelt struggles of the proud, hardworking poor of her time. Years later, Addie Tompkins, a resident of Cedar Grove, a small town on the Kanawha River, aptly commented, "that Mother Jones behaved like a woman who had replaced her past with zeal for what she was doing, as if she had already died and had nothing left to fear."[39] Always undaunted, she advocated for "her boys," the coal miners of the Mountain State.

Arriving in West Virginia in 1897, Mother Jones delivered speeches in Monongah and Flemington seeking to unionize miners. In Charleston, she, along with Samuel Gompers, head of the American Federation of Labor, and Eugene Debs, head of the American Railway Union during the Pullman Strike and now leader of the developing Socialist Party, addressed seventeen thousand striking miners and their supporters in a monster rally. As they continued their campaign to unionize workers, Debs and Jones became two of the most inspirational labor orators and influential socialists in American history.[40] Later, in the Kanawha Valley in 1902, Mother Jones continued her campaign to unionize seven thousand miners.

Known for organizing not only miners, but also their family members, Mother Jones instinctively understood the essential role that the wives of miners played in the company towns. "These women organized church activities so important to mining families… they played other roles as well as Bible instructors and tutors, singers, gardeners, seamstresses and laundresses, faith healers… they were the ones who transformed primitive coal camps into communities of working people…"[41] Understanding the cohesive nature of the family unit that was the life line of the company town, Mother Jones focused on men, women and children alike in their struggle for social justice.

It was in West Virginia in 1902 that Mother Jones was deemed to be "the most dangerous woman in in America" by U.S. District Attorney, Reese Blizzard. On trial for ignoring a court injunction that banned meetings by striking miners, Blizzard went on to say, "She comes into a state where peace and prosperity reign... crooks her little finger (and) twenty thousand contented men lay down their tools and walk out."[42] While Blizzard clearly exaggerated Mother Jones' ability to galvanize mine workers, her impact from the coal owner's perspective was ominously impressive.

Later, in the 1912 Paint Creek - Cabin Creek mining strike, union members and their families, evicted from company housing, set up tent colonies, demanding union recognition. Once again, Mother Jones arrived on the scene advocating for the miners and their families as a shooting war between UMWA strikers and a private army hired by mine owners escalated. Eventually, Governor William Glasscock imposed martial law, ordering 1,200 state militia to disarm both miners and mine guards.[43] Mother Jones was court martialed for inciting miners to riot and sentenced to twenty years confinement. However, she was released after eighty-five days of house arrest when Senator John Kern of Indiana began a Senate investigation into the local coal mines.

Newly sworn in Governor Henry Hatfield issued a series of terms for settlement of the strike, including a nine-hour work day (already in effect elsewhere in the state), the right to shop in stores other than those owned by the company, the right to elect union checkweighmen and the elimination of discrimination against union miners.[44] In April of 1913 after the governor ordered striking miners to accept these terms or be "deported" from the state, Paint Creek miners accepted these provisions while Cabin Creek miners continued the strike. Further violence ensued until July when Cabin Creek miners settled after the removal of mine guards from both Paint Creek and Cabin Creek was guaranteed. However, the right to organize as well as the right of collective bargaining remained unresolved. The Paint Creek-Cabin Creek strike brought new labor leaders to prominence: most notably, Frank Keeney, who became president of UMWA District 17, and Fred Mooney as the district's secretary-treasurer. Both men would play a prominent role as organizers of the 1921 march to Mingo County and subsequent Battle of Blair Mountain.

Mother Jones remained a staunch advocate for the coal miners of West Virginia. In a speech at a special convention of the UMWA, she applauds them saying, "...no state ever produced nobler, truer, better men under the appalling circumstances and conditions under which they work... Think of the New River field, of the Kanawha River... and think of the work the boys have done there."[45] Mother Jones identified so strongly with the miners of West Virginia that she announced to her fellow delegates, "I shall consider it an honor if, when you write my epitaph upon my tombstone, you say, 'Died fighting their battles in West Virginia.' "[46] To her boys in West Virginia, Mother Jones was truly the "Miner's Angel."

Although unionization remained problematic, the UMWA continued to fight for collective bargaining well into the twentieth century. In fact, West Virginia was the site of the most deadly strike violence in American history: the Battle of Blair Mountain in Logan County. From late August to September 4,

1921, in an attempt to unionize the southwestern coalfields of West Virginia, approximately 10,000 armed miners confronted over 3,000 lawmen and strikebreakers. What began as a march to Mingo County culminated in an all out battle at Blair Mountain that ended only after President Warren G. Harding at Governor Ephraim Morgan's request ordered 2,100 United States Army infantry to intervene. In her last trip to West Virginia, Mother Jones, fearful of the bloodshed that could ensue, had warned union leaders Frank Keeney and Fred Mooney not to pursue this protest against the mine owners. Still, the march progressed to Blair Mountain, as miners, including many veterans of the Spanish American War and World War I dressed in their worn doughboy uniforms, sang "a ditty" to the tune of *John Brown's Body*.[47]

In the violent conflict, Bill Blizzard, president of District 17 of the UMWA, commanded the miner's army against the forces led by Logan County Sheriff Don Chafin. However, the hostilities ended calmly when the federal troops arrived. The miners would not resist the United States Army in which so many of them had served.[48] Estimates of deaths varied to as many as one hundred, but after a detailed study of the march and the battle, on September 21, 1921, *Huntington Herald-Dispatch* journalist Lon Savage "concluded that sixteen men had died in the fighting, all but four of them miners."[49] Although no federal charges were filed,[50] multiple state trials followed. Most notably, Keeney and Mooney were tried and acquitted of murder charges. Ultimately, both men were forced out of the UMWA.[51] Ironically, due to a change of venue, Bill Blizzard, indicted for treason against West Virginia, was tried in the same courthouse where John Brown had been convicted of treason against Virginia in 1859. After several trials in different locations, all charges were dropped against Blizzard who remained a strong force in District 17 until his ouster in the 1950s. However, the defeat of the miners at Blair Mountain brought a temporary end to union efforts in southern West Virginia. Extensive court costs had depleted union coffers, and by 1924, membership in the UMWA in West Virginia dropped to one half of its 1921 total.[52]

Eventually, in 1933 as part of President Franklin Delano Roosevelt's New Deal legislation enacted in the First One Hundred Days, the passage of the National Industrial Recovery Act guaranteed the right of collective bargaining for unions. Later, the National Labor Relations Act of **1935 further strengthened** the right of workers to organize into trade unions to engage in collective bargaining and to use the strike as a means of a collective action if necessary. In addition, the Fair Labor Standards Act of 1938 introduced the forty-hour work week and established a national minimum wage. Despite FDR's problems with Supreme Court rulings on the constitutionality of some New Deal legislation, these laws ultimately protected unionization and collective bargaining principles.

Mother Jones also brought child labor to the national forum when she exposed this problem **in mines, mills and factories**. The census of 1900 had revealed that one sixth of American children under the age of sixteen were employed. Indeed, Bill Blizzard, commander of the Blair Mountain miners' army, began work as a ten year old **alongside** his father in a mine in Cabin Creek, West Virginia. Using the chant of "we want to go to school, not the mines," Jones helped to secure much needed national attention to this issue by assembling the 1903 Children's Crusade. Despite President Theodore Roosevelt's failure to meet with her, Mother

Jones organized a march from Philadelphia to Oyster Bay, New York to dramatize the plight of working children.

Jones and the United Mine Workers were not alone. As the Progressive and Socialist Parties as well as reformers in the Republican and Democratic Parties of the early twentieth century gained momentum, advocates for social justice were committed to ending child labor, especially in the coal mines and factories. Believing firmly in the right of a child to be a child and to receive an education, these reformers used the proven tool of the exposé to depict the cruel life that so many American children endured. In *The Bitter Cry of the Children* (1906), **John Spargo** describes a child's life in a coal mine in West Virginia.

> *In the bituminous mines of West Virginia, boys of nine or ten are frequently employed. I met one little fellow ten years old in Mt. Carbon, W. Va., last year, who was employed as a "trap boy."...what it means to be a trap boy at ten years of age... to sit alone in a dark mine passage hour after hour, with no human soul near; to see no living creature except the mules as they pass with their loads... to stand in water or mud that covers the ankles, chilled to the marrow by the cold draughts that rush in when you open the trap door for the mules to pass through; to work for fourteen hours - waiting - opening and shutting a door - then waiting again for sixty cents; to reach the surface when all is wrapped in the mantle of night... Boys twelve years of age may be legally employed in the mines of West Virginia, by day or by night... Where the disregard of child life is such that this may be done openly and with legal sanction, it is easy to believe what miners have again and again told me - that there are hundreds of little boys of nine*

and ten years of age employed in the coal mines of this state.[53]

For these young boys, life in the mining towns of West Virginia was difficult at best, giving great credence to Mother Jones' Children's Crusade cry of "we want school, not mines."

The plight of young boys working in the mines of West Virginia was further thrust into the national spotlight in the Fairmont Monongah Mining disaster of **December 6, 1907**. Not only was the nation appalled at the high death rate as a result of the explosions in the mines, but also that of the 361 fatalities, many were young boys. Although the Keating-Owen Act of 1916 outlawed child labor by prohibiting the sale in interstate commerce of goods produced in factories that employed children under fourteen or mines that employed children under sixteen, this law was short lived when it was declared unconstitutional in *Hammer vs. Dagenhart* nine months after its passage. It would not be until the enactment of the New Deal's Fair Labor Standards Act in 1938 that the rights of children in the workplace, factory or mine, would finally find this essential protection. In addition, while West Virginia had established compulsory education by 1897, enforcement remained problematic. It was only after a week's failure to attend school that absence might be investigated. True compulsory education would not become a reality until well into the twentieth century.[54]

Miners and their families lived in a rapidly developing industrial era replete with the complicating issues inherent in American society as a whole. As the wife of a miner and the teacher at the Coketon Colored School, Carrie Williams understood the realities of life for African Americans in their pursuit of the promise of the American dream, a dream premised on fairness and justice. At the same time, while she moved to Chicago after her husband's death in 1913, a year after the **Paint Creek - Cabin Creek** strike and years prior the Battle of Blair Mountain, Carrie Williams had to have been acutely aware of the miners' early efforts to unionize in West Virginia. As society struggled with both the legacy of slavery and the ongoing contentious relationship between miners and mine owners in the drama of unionization, Carrie Williams lived her life as a vibrant, caring member of her community. When she received her teaching contract that reduced the black school year to five months while retaining an eight-month calendar for white children, Carrie Williams challenged this gross inequity despite possible **negative consequences** for herself and her family in the company town of Coketon. Her subsequent victory in *Williams vs. the Tucker County Board of Education* ensuring a full academic year for black children in the Coketon Colored School and ultimately throughout the state of West Virginia is a testament to not only her courageous determination, but also her belief in the American system of justice.

1. "West Virginia's Mine Wars." *West Virginia Archives & History*, www.wvculture.org/history/archives/minewars.html.
2. Green, James R. *The Devil Is Here in These Hills: West Virginia's Coal Miners and Their Battle for Freedom.* New York, NY, Grove Press, 2015. p. 31.
3. Ibid.

4. "A Brief History of Coal and Health and Safety Enforcement in West Virginia." *West Virginia Office of Miners' Health Safety and Training*, 2002. www.wvminesafety.org/disaster.htm.
5. Ibid.
6. Green, James R. *The Devil Is Here in These Hills: West Virginia's Coal Miners and Their Battle for Freedom.* New York, NY, Grove Press, 2015. p. 14.
7. Ibid.
8. "West Virginia Coal Facts." *West Virginia Office of Miners' Health Safety and Training*, 2002, www.wvminesafety.org/disaster.htm.
9. "A West Virginia Timeline." jeff560.tripod.com/wv-hist.html.
10. "U.S. Census Bureau." *Department of Commerce*, www.commerce.gov/doc/us-census-bureau#4/37.91/-96.24.
11. Phillips, Cynthia A. *Images of Tucker County.* Charleston, SC, Arcadia Publishing, 2005. p. 65.
12. "African-American Population of Present-day West Virginia Counties in 1860 in West Virginia." *West Virginia Archives & History*, www.wvculture.org/history/archives/blacks/timeline.html.
13. "West Virginia Population by Race." *West Virginia Archives & History*, www.wvculture.org/history/teacherresources/censuspopulationrace.html
14. Blum, John M. *The National Experience: A History of the United States.* 8th ed., San Diego, New York, Chicago,

Atlanta, Washington D.C., London, Sydney, and Toronto, Cengage Learning, January 2, 1993. p. 428.
15. Ibid., p. 434.
16. Phillips, Cynthia A. *Images of Tucker County*. Charleston, SC, Arcadia Publishing, 2005. p. 73.
17. "A Brief History of Coal and Health and Safety Enforcement in West Virginia." *West Virginia Office of Miners' Health Safety and Training*, 2002. www.wvminesafety.org/disaster.htm.
18. Nutter, T. *Thomas, West Virginia: History, Progress and Development*. Parsons, W. Va., McClain Print. Co., 1906. p. 44.
19. Green, James R. *The Devil Is Here in These Hills: West Virginia's Coal Miners and Their Battle for Freedom*. New York, NY, Grove Press, 2015. p. 22.
20. Ibid., p. 21.
21. Ibid.
22. *Whipple Company Store & Museum*, Tour whipplecompanystore.com/ourstory.html.
23. Green, James R. *The Devil Is Here in These Hills: West Virginia's Coal Miners and Their Battle for Freedom*. New York, NY, Grove Press, 2015. p. 22.
24. Ibid.
25. "West Virginia's Mine Wars." *West Virginia Archives & History*, www.wvculture.org/history/archives/minewars.html.
26. Rice, Connie Park. "'Don't Flinch nor Yield an Inch': J. R. Clifford and the Struggle for Equal Rights in West

Virginia." *West Virginia History: A Journal of Regional Studies*, vol. 1, no. 2, 2008, p. 51.
27. Phillips, Cynthia A. *Images of Tucker County*. Charleston, SC, Arcadia Publishing, 2005. p. 65.
28. Green, James R. *The Devil Is Here in These Hills: West Virginia's Coal Miners and Their Battle for Freedom*. New York, NY, Grove Press, 2015. p. 25.
29. Ibid., p. 26.
30. Ibid.
31. Phillips, Cynthia A. *Images of Tucker County*. Charleston, SC, Arcadia Publishing, 2005. p. 62.
32. Browne, Allen. "Landmarks." *A Ghost Town in the Southwest Corner of Maryland*, 9, March, 2012, allenbrowne.blogspot.com/2012/03/upper-potomac-ghost-town-in-southwest.html.
33. "Davis Was a Cheapskate." Excerpt from *Appalachia: A History* by John Alexander Williams, 2002 *The Pioneer Press - Niagara Centennial Edition*, vol. 125, no. 1, 12 Aug. 2006. p. 4.
34. "Remarkable Career of the Late Henry Gassaway Davis." *B and O Magazine*, vol. 3, 1914. p. 38.
35. Wolfe, Eugene. "December 6, 1907 No Christmas at Monongah." *Goldenseal* Vol. 19, No. 4 West Virginia Traditional Life Winter. 1993. pp. 11-13.
36. Ibid., pp. 14-15.
37. Green, James R. *The Devil Is Here in These Hills: West Virginia's Coal Miners and Their Battle for Freedom*. New York, NY, Grove Press, 2015. p. 36.

38. Ibid., p. 37.
39. Ibid., p. 45.
40. Ibid., p. 40.
41. Ibid., p. 25.
42. "Reese L. Blizzard.", www.findagrave.com/cgi-in/fg.cgi?page=gr&GRid=23853606.
43. "West Virginia's Mine Wars." *West Virginia Archives & History*, www.wvculture.org/history/archives/minewars.html. p. 2.
44. Ibid.
45. Green, James R. *The Devil Is Here in These Hills: West Virginia's Coal Miners and Their Battle for Freedom.* New York, NY, Grove Press, 2015. p. 48.
46. Ibid., p. 41.
47. Ibid., p. 260.
48. Ibid., p. 282.
49. Ibid., p. 405.
50. Ibid., p. 284.
51. "West Virginia's Mine Wars." *West Virginia Archives & History*, www.wvculture.org/history/archives/minewars.html.
52. Ibid.
53. Spargo, John, *The Bitter Cry of the Children.* New York, The Macmillan Co. 1906. pp. 163-165.
54. Katz, Michael S. "A History of Compulsory Education Laws." *Fastback Series*, Vol. 75, Bicentennial Series, Phi Delta Kappa Foundation, 1976. p. 18.

CHAPTER FOUR
The Honorable Judge

The life of Justice Joseph Thatcher Hoke reflects the complicated threads of West Virginia's history. Born in Berkeley County, Virginia, on February 6, 1835, Hoke understood the intricacies of the Commonwealth's plantation based society, yet he became a staunch Unionist and proponent of assisting the freedmen and their families in their struggles to achieve a new status as citizens. As a leader in West Virginia, Hoke played a crucial role in the ratification of the 15th Amendment that secured the rights of citizenship for the freedmen. In addition, appreciating the necessity of education for African Americans, he obtained the charter for Storer College, providing a viable solution to the shortage of black teachers to educate the freedmen and their families. Later as the judge in *Williams vs. the Tucker County Board of Education of Fairfax District,* Hoke presided over what became a pivotal case in the struggle for fair access to educational opportunities for African Americans in West Virginia. His professional life depicts his values, particularly his sense of basic fairness that American law continues to translate into action.

Although a Virginian, Hoke spent much of his young life in northern states. He attended Rock River Seminary in Illinois and then studied at Oberlin College in Ohio before transferring to Hillsdale College in Michigan. Hoke's collegiate experience clearly impacted his societal views. Although founded in 1844 by the Freewill Baptists, Hillsdale College, originally named Michigan Central, has been officially nondenominational since its inception.[1] Most importantly, its charter prohibited any discrimination on the basis of race, religion or sex. Blacks were admitted immediately and Hillsdale became the second college in the United States to grant a four-year liberal arts degree to women, graduating the first woman in Michigan with a Bachelor of Arts in 1852.

A further influence was the key role that E.B. Fairfield, president of Hillsdale College from 1848 to 1869, played in the formation of the Republican Party. Along with Hillsdale Professor Ransom Dunn, he helped to found the new party and was present at its first convention in nearby Jackson, Michigan. Hillsdale College's early anti-slavery stance brought distinguished orators to the campus, including Frederick Douglass who visited the campus on two occasions as well as Edward Everett, the orator who preceded Abraham Lincoln at the dedication of the Soldiers' National Cemetery at Gettysburg. With the outbreak of the Civil War, a higher percentage of Hillsdale College students enlisted than that of any other institution of higher learning in what was then considered the western colleges. Of the more than five hundred volunteers from Hillsdale College, half became officers, including five lieutenant colonels and three generals. Included in the roster of Hillsdale volunteers are four recipients of the Medal of Honor.[2] In total, sixty Hillsdale students died in the conflict.

HON. JOSEPH T. HOKE, LL. D.

Image Source: Prominent Men of West Virginia

Desiring to make the law his career, after graduating from Hillsdale College in 1860, Hoke studied at the University of Michigan in Ann Arbor, earning a LL.B. in August of 1864. At this point, he returned to Martinsburg in the newly created West Virginia. Once home, he was commissioned by Governor A.I. Boreman to organize the first loyal civil government of the Union people in Berkeley and Jefferson Counties which elected officers for the area in October of 1864, assuring that this section would remain part of the young state. At that time, Governor Francis Pierpont of the Restored Government of Virginia sought to include these counties in Virginia. The governor later sought legal redress. However, in 1871, the United States Supreme Court recognized Berkeley and Jefferson Counties as part of West Virginia.

In 1864, Hoke was elected Prosecuting Attorney in addition to his appointment as Clerk of the Board of Supervisors of Berkeley County. A year later, he established a weekly newspaper, the *Berkeley Union*, in Martinsburg just prior to Lee's surrender at Appomattox Court House. This weekly newspaper was the first Republican paper printed in this section of the state. In 1870, Hoke merged the *Berkeley Union* with the *New Era*, resulting in the *Independent.* After moving to Keyser, West Virginia in 1876, he created the *Mountain Echo*, another Republican newspaper. Hoke was also awarded an honorary LL.D. from Hillsdale College in 1870.

In addition to his legal and newspaper careers, Hoke served in the West Virginia State Senate representing the 11th District composed of Berkeley and Jefferson Counties. Not surprisingly, he was deeply concerned about higher education in the new state. In 1866, as a senator and a member of the Board of Visitors of the State Agricultural College at Morgantown, he was instrumental in transforming the land grant college into West Virginia University. For several years, Hoke was a member and president of the university's Board of Regents and assisted in the initial planning of the curriculum as well as selecting its first faculty. Likewise, then fellow State Senator Henry Gassaway Davis collaborated with Hoke in his efforts to establish West Virginia University.

Reelected to the State Senate in 1868, Hoke was chairman of the Judiciary Committee and a leading proponent of the ratification of 15th Amendment that extended the right to vote to African American men. As Atkinson and Gibbens attest in the 1890 *Prominent Men of West Virginia,* "But for his (Hoke's) energetic efforts that amendment most likely would not have been ratified. Many Republican members were opposed to it, some of whom Judge Hoke induced to remain out of the Senate and not vote against it. Others he persuaded to vote for it; and withal the Joint Resolution was only adopted by 10 to 8, there being only three Democrats in the Senate at that time."[3] Interestingly, his colleague and future owner of Davis Coal and Coke Company, Democratic Senator Henry Gassaway Davis regarded enfranchising African American men as "a grave mistake." Instead, he chose to exert his influence on behalf of ex-Confederates who were forced to take loyalty oaths in order to achieve normal participation in government and economic pursuits.[4]

One of Hoke's greatest senate accomplishments was securing a charter for Storer College (also referred to as Storer Normal College) at Harper's Ferry in Jefferson County for the education of African Americans in West Virginia. Similar to Hillsdale, Storer College shared roots with the Freewill Baptists. During the Civil War, this religious group had established a national missionary effort to educate the newly freed slaves. While

Prosecuting Attorney in Berkeley County from 1864 to 1866, Hoke boarded Freewill Baptist missionary teachers in his home in Martinsburg. Furthermore, in his role as local legal counsel for the Freewill Baptists and as a member of the Baptist Commission for the Promotion of Education in the South, he helped the Baptists write Storer College's charter.[5] Not only did Senator Hoke advocate for the passage of this charter, but also he cast the deciding vote to incorporate the college.

Founded in 1867, Storer College was the response to the overwhelming need for African American teachers to educate the newly freed slaves. Earlier in 1865, Reverend Nathan Brackett, a Freewill Baptist and staunch abolitionist whose family roots were in the Shenandoah Valley, had established a black primary school in the Lockwood House at Harper's Ferry. This effort, in conjunction with other philanthropic organizations as well as the Freedman's Bureau, attempted to provide a basic education to former slaves. However, Brackett and fellow philanthropists soon faced an overwhelming problem.

At the end of the Civil War, more than 30,000 newly freed people were congregated in the Shenandoah Valley alone. Relatively few of them were from area plantations. Most had come north with the Union Army, seeking some form of refuge. However, the overall crisis was far more dramatic. As early as January 1865, some estimates report that 750 persons were teaching 75,000 black children in Union-held territory throughout the South.[6] Shepherd University historian John Stealey aptly summarized the conclusions of the Freewill Baptists and other philanthropists. "As they dealt with relief, as they dealt with the refugee situation, as they dealt with education, the Free Will Baptists soon realized that the problem was too large to deal with. Their solution was to create a normal school to teach blacks to teach blacks."[7] That realization resulted in the creation of Storer Normal School.

A turning point occurred when Brackett's Lockwood House School came to the attention of John Storer, a philanthropist from Maine. Storer provided a grant of $10,000 to establish a school on three conditions. First of all, the school must eventually become a degree-granting institution; and secondly, it must be open to all applicants regardless of race or gender. While these prerequisites did not present significant problems, the final condition requiring that the Freewill Baptist Church match the donated funds within the year did present a serious obstacle. However, with great difficulty, the Freewill Baptists raised the necessary money and the Storer Normal School (later Storer College) received its state charter due to Hoke's efforts in the state senate.

Reverend Brackett became the first president of the only school in West Virginia that offered education above the elementary level to African Americans. Initially, Storer had a faculty of two teachers and a student body of nineteen. By 1890, enrollment had increased to two hundred and fifty students. Although the Freewill Baptists attempted to continue to fund Storer, eventually the state government provided the necessary funding.[8] The once one-room Lockwood House School was now Storer College, a full-fledged degree granting institution open to both men and women of all races and creeds. Among the trustees of Storer College were Justice Joseph Hoke and E.B. Fairfield, president of Hillsdale College in Michigan.

The initial reaction of many of the people in Harper's Ferry to Storer College was less than welcoming. Numerous local residents were Confederate sympathizers who saw Storer as a "colored school with nigger teachers."[9] From slander to vandalism to assault, many townspeople fought to rid their town of this educational blight. One teacher wrote, "It is unusual for me to go to the post office without being hooted at and twice I have been stoned on the streets at noonday."[10] Harassment and vandalism continued for several years as teachers and students received frequent visits from cadets on leave from the Virginia Military Institute in Lexington, Virginia, as well as intrusions into the schoolrooms by locals attempting to intimidate faculty and students alike.[11] However, these tactics failed and eventually Harper's Ferry accepted its new neighbor, even regarding their fellow citizen Reverend Brackett with respect. It was not until 1944 when Storer College inaugurated its first black president, Richard McKinney, that prejudice again dramatically appeared on the scene. President McKinney was welcomed to Harper's Ferry with a burning cross in his yard.[12]

Originally founded as a normal school to educate teachers, over the course of its history, Storer College expanded its curriculum to include four-year degree programs as well as an industrial program for skilled laborers. Although Storer officially became a four-year college in 1938, it was never formally accredited. Enrollment peaked at approximately three hundred students. After the Supreme Court decision in the *Brown vs. Board of Education, Topeka, Kansas* case deemed segregated schools unconstitutional, West Virginia withdrew its financial support from the college. The state government did continue to fund two other historically black state institutions of higher learning: Bluefield State College and West Virginia State University. Storer College closed its historic doors in 1955.

The importance of Storer College cannot be overstated. In the immediate post Civil War era, many missionary groups had flocked to the deep South to provide educational opportunities for the newly freed slaves. In an interview in the West Virginia Memory Project, historian Ancella Bickley states, "that did not happen in West Virginia, and so Storer College is... one of a kind... providing in its own right... educational help for people in the eastern panhandle and probably other points north of that in West Virginia... (Storer) is a marvelous example of a cooperative effort in West Virginia between the Freedman's Bureau, the church and black people themselves who were interested in education there."[13]

Another unique feature of Storer College is its understanding that the former slaves needed more than mere literacy. The first college catalog advises that students were to "receive counsel and sympathy, learn what constitutes correct living and become qualified for the performance of the great work of life." Storer College also demanded that students "give satisfactory evidence of good moral character" and abide by the school's "established codes of conduct" complete with educational and social prohibitions that included no attendance at balls, dances, or parties without permission, and only on weekends; no visiting drinking saloons or imbibing of intoxicating liquors; no using profane or indecent language; no card playing, jumping, dancing or fighting in buildings; and no smoking on the school grounds or public streets.[14] Added to this was the expectation that Storer students would, in turn, educate their home communities. As the legacy of slavery unfolded, black teachers had a personal understanding of the cultural and historical implications of life for their students, enhancing the role that African Americans played in their schools and communities.

As an educational institution that prepared black teachers to teach black children, Storer College responded not only to a desperate educational need, but it also became a source of professional opportunities for the African American community. Indeed, many prominent black West Virginia families started as teachers. For example, John Robert Clifford, a graduate of Storer College and the first African American lawyer admitted to the West Virginia bar, earned his teaching degree at this institution. Later, he successfully represented Carrie Williams in her suit against the Tucker County Board of Education of Fairfax District that had shortened the length of the colored school year to five months while keeping the white schools in session for eight months. It is an historical irony that this case was tried before Judge Hoke who had been instrumental in obtaining the state charter for Storer College and remained as a long-term trustee of the institution.

The physical setting of Storer College also holds a unique place in American history. Its campus quite literally sits within the federal arsenal made so famous by John Brown's Raid. On May 30, 1881, Frederick Douglass, who also spoke at Hillsdale College, Judge Hoke's alma mater, delivered a speech at Storer College in which he praised the efforts of John Brown to free the slaves and make abolition a national cause. Seated behind Douglass on the platform was the district attorney who twenty-two years earlier had successfully prosecuted Brown for treason against the Commonwealth of Virginia. Like Judge Hoke, Douglass was a member of the Storer College Board of Trustees.

In August of 1906, Storer College hosted the second conference of the Niagara Movement. Rejecting Booker T. Washington's Atlanta Compromise that promoted the theory of accommodation to gain social equality, the members of the Niagara Movement demanded full civil rights and an end to segregation. J. R. Clifford, a founder of this group, arranged and hosted the conference at his alma mater. Leaders of this historic meeting included W.E.B. Du Bois, John Hope, and William Monroe Trotter. As Secretary of the West Virginia Branch of the Niagara Movement, Clifford delivered the opening address which was followed by his sixteen-year old daughter Mary's recitation of Du Bois' *Credo*: "I believe in God who made of one blood all races that dwell on earth... black and brown and white are brothers... Especially do I believe in the Negro Race, in the beauty of its genius, the sweetness of its soul and its strength in meekness... I believe in Liberty for all men;... the right to vote... I believe in the training of children black even as white... Life lit by some large vision of beauty and goodness and truth."[15]

In addition to the meetings and seminars, members of the Niagara Movement took part in a morning barefoot vigil in John Brown's cell to honor what they regarded as the hallowed ground of the man who led the failed attempt to free the slaves. Participants concluded by singing *The Battle Hymn of the Republic,* a favorite marching song of the Union Army.[16] While Julia Ward Howe used the original music of *John Brown's Song (later John Brown's Body),* her 1862 lyrics evoke an evangelical reckoning at the end of the war. However, by the conclusion of the Civil War, the words had reverted to the earlier version of *John Brown's Body,* emphatically stating, *"His soul's marching on,"* now along with the members of the Niagara Movement and later with the striking miners in the 1921 Battle of Blair Mountain.[17] Du Bois later described the Storer conference as one of the greatest meetings that American Negroes ever held.

Leaders of the Niagara Movement
W. E. B. Du Bois (seated), and (left to right) J. R. Clifford,
L. M. Hershaw, and F. H. M. Murray at Harpers Ferry.
Source: National Park Service

Through its unwavering commitment to full citizenship and equal rights, the goals of the Niagara Movement became the cornerstone of the twentieth century civil rights movement. However, due to internal divisions, by 1910 the organization had dissolved. Eventually, the Niagara Movement evolved into the National Association for the Advancement of Colored People, the NAACP. At this time, Clifford broke with the group because, among other disagreements, he objected to the use of "colored" in the organization's title.[18]

Just as Joseph Hoke's commitment to Storer College was an integral part of his life's work, so too was his lifelong public service to West Virginia. In addition to his tenure in the state senate, Hoke served as a delegate to the Republican National Conventions in 1868, 1872 and 1880. Then, due to his wife's frail health, he moved to Kingwood in Preston County in 1881. Here, Hoke represented his county for two years in the West Virginia House of Delegates from 1886 to 1888. At the end of this term, Hoke was elected a Judge of the Third Judicial Circuit. It was in this capacity that Judge Hoke presided over the *Carrie Williams* case.

Judge Joseph Thatcher Hoke could not have known when he transferred to Hillsdale College the critical role that he would play in the civil rights history of West Virginia. His presence on a campus alive with antislavery beliefs and a college president actively engaged in the birth of the Republican Party must have been a formative influence on him. Upon his return to West Virginia, Hoke found himself in a pivotal position as a senator in the newly formed state. His advocacy of the ratification of the 15th Amendment was crucial. Furthermore, in securing a charter for Storer College, he could not foresee the impact that this institution would have. What he did see was a dramatic need that he sought to address. Again, Hoke could not predict that he would preside over *Williams vs. the Tucker County Board of Education of Fairfax District*, a case argued by Clifford, a graduate of Storer College and a civil rights proponent.

Throughout his professional life, Judge Hoke translated his beliefs into actions that positively affected opportunities for African Americans in West Virginia. Like many of his contemporaries, he often expressed himself in poetry.

> We write but a line,
> We leave but a name,
> We cast but a leaf on the tide;
> The line is soon gone,
> The name is soon blank,
> The leaf with the current will glide.
>
> Thus ever like leaves,
> Of the beautiful spring,
> In youth time we shadow the deep,
> But soon, like the leaves
> Of the autumn, we fall,
> And float on the billows asleep.[19]

While Justice Hoke speaks of the transience of the human condition here, his life's work endures in its positive impact on the lives of so many of his fellow citizens. Although integrated schools would not be achieved for many years, the *Williams* case guaranteed an equal school year for the African American children of West Virginia as well as equal pay for their teachers. Hoke's role in promoting fair access to educational opportunities remains a fitting testament to his character and his belief in the rule of law in the Great American Experiment.

1. "History." *Hillsdale College*, www.hillsdale.edu/about/history/.
2. Ibid.
3. Atkinson, George Wesley, and Alvaro Franklin Gibbens. *Prominent Men of West Virginia*. Wheeling, W. Va., W.L. Collin, 1890. pp. 456-457.
4. Pepper, Charles M. *The Life and Times of Henry Gassaway Davis*. New York, NY, The Century Co., 1920. p. 44.
5. Rice, Connie Park. "'Don't Flinch or Yield an Inch': J. R. Clifford and the Struggle for Equal Rights in West Virginia." *West Virginia History: A Journal of Regional Studies*, vol. 1, no. 2, 2008, p. 52.
6. Gozdzik Ph.D, Gloria. "A Historic Resource for Storer College at Harpers Ferry, West Virginia." N*ps.gov/Parkhistory/online_books/Hafe/Storer.pdf*, Jan. 2002. p. 19.
7. Fisher, Emma. "Storer College." *The Pioneer Press - Niagara Centennial Edition*, vol. 125, no. 1, 12 Aug. 2006. p. 5.
8. "Storer College: It Was Here a Century Ago That the NAACP Took Its First Steps." *The Journal of Blacks in Higher Education*, no. 51, 2006, p. 21.
9. Ibid.
10. Ibid.
11. Rice, Connie Park. "'For Men and Measures: The Life and Legacy of Civil Rights Pioneer J.R. Clifford." *Eberly College of Arts and Sciences at West Virginia University*, 2007. p. 28.
12. "Storer College: It Was Here a Century Ago that the NAACP Took Its First Steps." *The Journal of Blacks in Higher Education*, No. 51, 2006, p. 22.

13. *Transcript of Interview with Ancella Bickley, June 21, 1992, for the Film "West Virginia."* www.wvculture.org/history/wvmemory/filmtranscripts/wvbickley.html p.12.
14. "Storer College Catalog 1869." *West Virginia Archives & History*, www.wvculture.org/history/education/storercatalog1869.html. pp. 10-11.
15. "Mary Clifford Reads *The Credo* at Niagara." *Pioneer Press – The Souvenir Edition*. 2004-2006, www.jrclifford.org/images/JR%20Clifford%20and%20the%20Carrie%20Williams%20Case.pdf. p. 24.
16. "J.R. Clifford at Niagara." Excerpt from *W.E.B. Du Bois: Biography of a Race, 1868-1919*, by David Levering Lewis, 1993. *Pioneer Press – The Souvenir Edition*. 2004-2006, www.jrclifford.org/images/JR%20Clifford%20and%20the%20Carrie%20Williams%20Case.pdf. p. 24.
17. Green, James R. *The Devil Is Here in These Hills: West Virginia's Coal Miners and Their Battle for Freedom*. New York, NY, Grove Press, 2015. p. 260.
18. "J. R. Clifford." *West Virginia Archives & History*, www.wvculture.org/history/archives/blacks/clifford.html.
19. Atkinson, George Wesley, and Alvaro Franklin Gibbens. *Prominent Men of West Virginia*. Wheeling, W. Va., W.L. Collin, 1890. p. 458.

CHAPTER FIVE
Educator and Protector

When Carrie Williams challenged the Tucker County Board of Education of Fairfax District's order curtailing the school term for African American children, she was confronting not only a contemporary injustice, but also the societal repercussions resulting from the history of black education in Virginia prior to the Civil War. As West Virginia became the thirty-fifth state admitted to the Union, it too shared in the legacy of slavery and the subsequent struggle for fair access to educational opportunities for African Americans. The power of education as the ultimate source of true freedom is a core value, one long recognized as a necessity in the national experience. For Carrie Williams, education was the conduit to genuine participation in American democracy. Protecting and extending equal educational opportunities for the black children of West Virginia was a battle that she determinedly chose to fight.

As slavery became increasingly entrenched in Virginia, efforts to prevent the education of African Americans gained momentum. Earlier in 1819, the House of Burgesses had revised the Virginia Slave Code, outlawing the education of both slaves and free blacks. At the judge's discretion, the corporal punishment for those convicted of violating this section of the Revised Code was not to exceed twenty lashes. Despite this prohibition during what is considered the Pioneer Period prior to the Civil War, some "benevolent" slave masters attempted to provide slaves who had served them well with "a modicum of knowledge."[1] Others, believing in the necessity of education for all, sought to foster some form of education for blacks. According to the Virginia Code, while schools were banned, private tutoring was permissible. Teaching slaves or free blacks to read and write took place fairly widely in the private sphere, but so too did the punishment of teacher and student alike.[2]

However, Nat Turner's Rebellion in 1831 only fueled the drive for complete eradication of educational opportunities for blacks. Turner, a literate slave, led a rebellion of slaves and free blacks in Southampton County, Virginia, resulting in the execution of fifty-five of his supporters as well as Turner's subsequent trial, conviction and hanging. State legislators moved quickly to pass legislation that further prohibited the education of all blacks, slave and free. Despite this legal prohibition, by 1835, twelve cases unsuccessfully challenged the 1819 Code and subsequent laws. Among the earliest organized attempts to educate African Americans occurred in Wheeling where John Templeton, John Moore, Stanley Cuthbert and Ellen Ritchie were charged with illegally teaching blacks to read.[3] As late as 1854, Margaret Douglass, a white seamstress who also conducted a school for free black children in Norfolk, Virginia, spent a month in jail for violating the Virginia Code.[4] Resistance to the education of free blacks in the state found new support in the Virginia Code of 1860 forbidding free African Americans who were educated in other states to return to the Commonwealth. These early efforts to educate African American children, slave or free, as well as the ensuing stringent response highlight the underlying tension that was brewing within Virginia.

As the Second Wheeling Convention reconvened to draft a constitution for the new state of West Virginia on November 26, 1861, African Americans in Parkersburg sought an end to the existing cycle of illiteracy by seeking educational opportunities for their children. A prominent leader in this effort was Robert W. Simmons, who visited Lincoln during the Civil War seeking assistance to establish a desperately needed school. Other activists included Thomas Furguson, Charles Hicks, William Sergeant, William Smith, Matthew Thomas, Robert Thomas and Lafayette Wilson. As these advocates struggled to find educational solutions, their aim was twofold: to foster a sense of African American identity and to centralize authority within the black community. Creating the Colored School Board in January of 1862, they established the first public school for African Americans in West Virginia. Initially, this 1862 effort resulted in a pay school housed in the basement of a white church and taught by a white minister, S. E. Colburn. Tuition was a dollar per month with provisions to help students whose families could not pay the fee.[5]

As the Parkersburg model evolved, it quickly became not only tuition free, but also the first school established for black youth south of the Mason-Dixon Line and the only one manned by African American men in the United States, except for the Gaines High School in Cincinnati, Ohio.[6] Eventually, the Parkersburg school became the Sumner School named for the Radical Republican Senator of Massachusetts, Charles Sumner, an abolitionist who was committed to ensuring equal rights for the freedmen during Reconstruction. Blacks also spearheaded educational opportunities in Wheeling and later in Cabell County, sometimes using rented spaces as makeshift schools. The Parkersburg method of establishing schools where African Americans retained centralized authority soon became the preferred black educational model followed in other areas of West Virginia.

When the first state legislature met in 1863, the education of "free colored children" was approved, but was not funded. Reporting to the legislature in 1864, the State Superintendent of Public Schools admonished that blacks had been "too long and too mercilessly neglected of this (education) privilege."[7] By 1867, the West Virginia Legislature provided schools for African Americans ages six through twenty-one in districts where there were more than fifteen black students.[8]

Later in 1872, the revised state constitution affirmed the commitment to black education but with the condition that black and white education must be segregated. Although loyal to the Union during the Civil War and later closely linked to northern industrialists, much of West Virginia continued to share social mores with its southern neighbors.[9] While most school boards cooperated with state mandates, at times coercion or court action had to be taken in order to provide African American children with proper education. By the late 19th century, the number of students needed was lowered to ten, allowing districts to establish more schools for black children.[10]

While much of the defeated South received the attention of missionaries and the Freedman's Bureau, West Virginia, for the most part, did not experience this outside intervention.[11] However, missionaries did bring much needed zeal to the statewide need to educate blacks. Often setting up crude classrooms in "shanty-like school-houses," these activists proclaimed the power of education as the great leverage by which the recently emancipated race could achieve genuine recognition in the national experience.[12] Although the Freedmen's Bureau sought to assist African Americans, the end result was somewhat detrimental to blacks. According to historian Stephen Engle, "Ironically, the Freeman's Bureau to some degree hurt black institutions... such as schools, since it ultimately placed them under white control. Leaders within black communities of Charleston and Parkersburg, intolerant of white domination in their educational matters, actively protested white control."[13] Under these circumstances, African Americans believed that while black leadership could emerge, it could do so "only with white acquiescence or support."[14]

Consequently, using the Parkersburg model to centralize educational authority within the black community, African Americans sought greater control over the education of their children. Progressive black leaders such as Thomas Furguson, William Sergeant and Robert Thomas, among others, worked tirelessly in politics throughout the Reconstruction era and beyond to translate their commitment to black educational opportunities into reality for African American children.[15] Realizing that integrated schools were not a possibility, black leaders exerted political leverage to ensure that African American administrators and staff would be appointed to operate the state's segregated educational institutions.[16] Although dual school systems were expensive, blacks did not suffer from underfunding as did their counterparts in the South and the former Civil War border states. Interestingly, in the early twentieth century, funding for black schools exceeded that of money spent on white schools. West Virginia spent more per pupil for black students ($111.47) than for white students ($100.63).[17]

Since teachers were paid based upon qualifications, not race, black teachers fared well in West Virginia. Many capable young blacks entered the teaching profession, resulting in an African American middle class within the state. For example, after graduating from Storer College, J. R. Clifford was a teacher and principal of the Sumner School in Martinsburg prior to his legal practice. Earlier in his career, Clifford "had expressed doubts about integrated schools, claiming that some newspapers "...advocated 'mixed schools' a quarter of a century ahead of time" and that "thousands of people who depended on teaching for a living will not recover."[18] However, years later troubled by the persistent inequities that existed in segregated education, Clifford challenged this system in court.[19]

With the development of the timber and coal industries as well as the building and operation of the railroads in the post Civil War period, West Virginia experienced an influx of African Americans seeking employment in the Mountain State. Prior to the Civil War in 1860, approximately 21,144 blacks lived in what would become West Virginia. Of that number approximately 2,773 were free and 18,371 were slave.[20] However, by 1870, the African American population numbered only 17,980, largely due to the departure of slave owners into Confederate areas of control when the conflict commenced. Later, as blacks migrated to the Mountain State, these numbers changed dramatically. By 1880, African Americans numbered 25,886 with this segment of the population increasing to 64,173 by 1910 and to 114,893 by 1930.[21] Consequently, this population growth resulted in greater demands on the black educational system within the state.

African Americans saw life in the mining towns of West Virginia as a definite alternative to the impoverished agrarian economy of the New South. Inherent in this viewpoint was the hope of securing their share of the promise of the American dream and an essential aspect of that dream was access to the education that is so vital for overall success. By 1902, West Virginia had two hundred and seven black schools with two hundred and seventy-eight teachers serving 7,886 students.[22] Black miners clearly valued educational opportunities for their children. In 1910, nearly 80 percent of the black children in McDowell County attended school compared to 75 percent of native-white children in the same age bracket.[23] In response to the growing black student population, in 1919, West Virginia established the position of State Supervisor of Negro Schools and appointed a Negro Board of Education.[24] By 1930, a larger percentage of black youths in West Virginia attended high school than their counterparts in the southern or former border states.[25]

However, secondary educational opportunities for African Americans evolved gradually. The first high school was the Sumner School in Parkersburg that added secondary level courses in 1885. By 1923, West Virginia had twenty-one high schools for black children with some counties allowing students to attend high school outside of their district. For example, Preston County students attended high schools in Monongalia

County. Other educational options included boarding with families near a high school or traveling long distances by train, car or bus to attend school.

The poignant story of Doris Green illustrates this dilemma. A student at the Coketon Colored School near Thomas, West Virginia where Carrie Williams had successfully challenged the shortened school term for black children, Doris Green started her education in 1939. When she completed elementary school, her only option for high school was to relocate to a city far removed from her home and family. "Our daddy wouldn't let his girls go away to school. Back then colored kids had to go away to Clarksburg or Elkins to attend High School because there wasn't one for colored children… The only way they were able to go is if they had people there that they could stay with and find them a job."[26] Understandably, Doris' father did not want either of these options: Elkins is 36.5 miles from Coketon while Clarksburg is 65.5 miles away. But Doris loved learning, so her solution was to continue attending class at the Coketon Colored School. Even though Doris kept taking the "same grade over," she recounts, "I was always glad that it (Coketon Colored School) was there for us."[27]

As more African Americans sought higher educational opportunities, the state of West Virginia allocated more funds to black colleges. In addition to funding for Storer College that for twenty-five years had been the only in-state institution to train African American teachers, by 1913-1914, the state government spent 18 percent of the total state appropriations for higher education to fund the two relatively new black state colleges. These colleges, West Virginia Colored Institute founded in 1881 (now West Virginia State University) and Bluefield Colored

Institute established in 1895 (now Bluefield State College) served 5.3 percent of the state's overall population.[28] Many of these students were the children of miners. In the 1932-33 freshman class at West Virginia State, over 50 percent of these students were the sons and daughters of coal miners and other unskilled workers while at Bluefield State 93.9 percent of the 232 students were the children of coal miners.[29] Given the lack of high schools for so many black children, these colleges also offered secondary education to students.

Just as the founders of Storer College understood the dramatic need for African American teachers, so too did the black administrators and teachers in the growing number of "colored" schools, as increasingly blacks found employment in the new industries of the Mountain State. Consequently, the shortage of African American teachers in West Virginia provided the impetus for black teachers to migrate to the state. While some came from Virginia and Maryland, Ohio provided the greatest number of black teachers. Although African Americans attended integrated schools in Ohio, underlying racial prejudice still prevented black teachers from instructing white children in public schools.[30] West Virginia, on the other side of the Ohio River, was an oasis of opportunity for these teachers.

One such teacher was Caroline M. Edwards who was born in Chillicothe, Ohio, around 1866. Unfortunately, family background information is relatively limited. Carrie's parents, Jacob and Rachel, were both born in Virginia: Jacob around 1826 and Rachel between 1832 and 1838. However, it is not known if Carrie's parents were free or slave.[31] Similarly, while it is probable that they had other children, it is difficult to document. What is known is that at some point, the Edwards family settled in Chillicothe, Ohio where Carrie was raised and educated, most likely earning a normal school degree that qualified her as a teacher.

Carrie Williams
Courtesy of her descendant, Curtis Smith

The Edwards family choice of Chillicothe as their new home is revealing in itself. Originally a Shawnee settlement, after the

American Revolution, settlers from Virginia, including what would become West Virginia as well as Kentucky, moved west along the Ohio River to this section of Ohio in search of land. At two points in the history of Ohio, Chillicothe served as the capital until 1816 when Columbus, with its more centralized location, became the permanent capital of the state. Chillicothe became a center for both freedmen and escaped slaves where they created a vibrant community with fewer restrictions than in other areas near what would become the Confederate and border states.

As prewar conflicts heightened, Chillicothe's black population as well as white abolitionists played an essential role in manning stations of the Underground Railroad. Geographically, this area of Ohio provided the necessary refuge for slaves who fled across the Ohio River and then travelled northward on the Scioto River, creating a greater distance from their former homes and eluding fugitive slave hunters from as close as Cabell County in Virginia (later West Virginia) and Boone and Bourbon Counties in Kentucky. As West Virginia historian Ancella Bickley aptly states, "the Ohio River was literally the gateway to freedom. If you were an escaping slave and could get to the Ohio, you.... knew if you could get to the other side that there would be people who would take you in and help you move farther north and to absolute freedom."[32] Chillicothe's location on the Scioto River provided this essential northward access on the Underground Railroad for refugees escaping slavery.

In effect, the Ohio River became the critical first step to freedom ultimately to be found in Canada. Crossing this "Jordan" was made at almost any point where a boat could be found.[33] Although escaped slaves initially joined free blacks in northern and western Ohio, southern Michigan, Indiana and Illinois, raids by slave holders increasingly intensified. In 1847 and later in 1849, slave hunters from Kentucky unsuccessfully raided parts of Cass County, Michigan. In response to early fugitive slave laws, individual states had enacted "personal liberty laws" that did not require their citizens or officials to comply with warrants of agents of slave owners.

However, as conflicting beliefs between the North and the South intensified, the Fugitive Slave Act, included as part of the Compromise of 1850, served to make the work of the Underground Railroad more dangerous as well as clarifying the ultimate destination to be Canada. Nicknamed the "Bloodhound Law" because of the dogs used to hunt down fugitives, this new act required state officials and citizens of free states to cooperate in the return of escaped slaves. Many years before the *Carrie Williams* case, a young Henry Gassaway Davis stood in the overcrowded chamber of the United States Senate, witnessing the intense debate that this law engendered. At this point, Davis could not foresee the role that his future company, Davis Coal & Coke, would play in the education of young African American children in Coketon, West Virginia.

After the passage of the Compromise of 1850, arriving on the western side of the Ohio River was now the first step on a longer journey into possible freedom. Once in Ohio, active agents of the Underground Railroad provided a zigzag network of movement northward that helped escaped slaves reach Toledo, Sandusky (Ohio) and Detroit, where abolitionist ship captains and workers helped them reach Canada across Lake Erie and Lake Huron. Although some captains unknowingly transported escaped slaves, many were fervent abolitionists such as Captain Willibur of the *Michigan* who welcomed a band of fugitives onto his ship in

Sandusky with the greeting, "Well, I wish all Kentucky was aboard." In addition to trails and roads, agents of the Underground Railroad used actual railroads and canals to transport escaped slaves. Nineteenth century historian Wilbur Siebert estimated that thousands of miles of multiple trails existed in Ohio alone to assist refugees. These circuitous routes northward were deliberately designed to thwart fugitive slave hunters who were more likely to follow known routes between cities.[34]

Added to this strategic geographic importance, towns near the Ohio and Scioto Rivers provided a vibrant portrait of life where free blacks owned land and businesses and actively participated in the day-to-day life of their communities. Coincidentally, William Monroe Trotter, who established *The Boston Guardian,* a black newspaper, and together with J. R. Clifford and W.E.B. Du Bois co-founded the Niagara Movement, was born on his grandparents' farm in Chillicothe on April 7, 1872. Trotter's maternal ancestry stems from the enslaved families at Thomas Jefferson's home at Monticello. Years earlier, Trotter's grandfather, Tucker Isaacs, a free black, purchased the freedom of his grandmother, Ann-Elizabeth Fossett, a slave on the well known plantation. Subsequently, the family moved to Chillicothe where Trotter's mother Virginia was raised, eventually marrying James Trotter, a freed slave from Mississippi. The couple lived briefly in Boston after the Civil War only to return to Ohio for the birth of their son. While William Monroe Trotter's parents again relocated to Boston shortly after his birth, his early family roots in this section of Ohio reflect the possibilities that Chillicothe held for African Americans seeking a life outside of the antebellum South.

However, Ohio, similar to other northern areas, did not initially provide educational opportunities for blacks. By 1853, the state mandated that boards of education provide schools for African American children in districts having more than twenty students. Still, not surprisingly, on the eve of the Civil War, after studying African American schools across the state, Ohio's Commissioner of Public Schools reported that black schools were grossly unequal to white schools.[35] Despite this inequity, prior to the Civil War, higher educational opportunities existed for blacks as early as the 1820s at Western Reserve University and Ohio University as well as later at Antioch University (1852), Otterbein College (1853), Central State University (1856) and Wilberforce University (1856). Indeed, as early as 1835, Oberlin College, created in 1833, actively recruited black students. Judge Joseph Hoke briefly attended Oberlin College before transferring to Hillsdale College, also open to African Americans, in Michigan. Although many in Ohio believed slavery to be inherently wrong and were actively involved in abolition movements, others, particularly in southern sections of the state, allied themselves with southern sympathies. In fact, at the state constitutional convention in 1851, the assembly rejected enfranchising black men by a vote of 66 to 12.[36]

Chillicothe remains the only city in rural Ross County as well as its county seat. Five soldiers from this county were awarded the Medal of Honor for their service in the American Civil War.[37] This is the home community where Rachel and Jacob Edwards raised young Caroline, "Carrie," in the years following the Civil War. Again, while it is difficult to document, it is likely that her education and early teaching experience occurred in this section of Ohio. The strength and vibrancy of this community, black and white, must have impacted young Carrie.

At some point, Carrie Edwards moved to West Virginia where she married Abraham L. Williams on November 20, 1889, in Thomas, West Virginia, home of Davis Coal and Coke Company. Abraham was born in 1861 in Mineral County to Benjamin and Henrietta Williams. Carrie and Abraham had nine children: May (1891), Nevada (1892), Robert (1893), Russell (1897), Irving (1899), Ethel (1901), Josephine (1907), Juanita (1908) and Wendell Phillips Williams (1913). Nevada died during the influenza/pneumonia pandemic of 1918 and is buried in an unmarked grave in the Rose Hill Cemetery in Thomas. Abraham died in 1913, most likely from black lung disease. Carrie and her younger children, and later Nevada's children, then joined her older sons in Chicago where she lived until her death on January 22, 1930.[38]

Prior to the *Williams vs. Tucker County Board of Education of the Fairfax District* case, Carrie had taught for nearly ten years in Ohio and West Virginia, including several years at the Coketon Colored School.[39] The African American population in this area had risen dramatically due to the success of the Davis Coal and Coke Company and the expansion of the West Virginia Central & Pittsburg Railroad, another Davis enterprise. In a short period, the black population had grown significantly from 183 in 1890 to 253 in 1900. The majority of this African American population lived in Coketon, also headquarters of Davis Coal and Coke Company.[40] Similar to his other mining ventures, Henry Gassaway Davis and his management team were actively involved in all aspects of this company town from assigning housing and choosing land donated for churches as well as selecting the manager of the Buxton and Landstreet Store, the company emporium where miners used D C & C Co. coins to buy necessary goods. Principals and teachers in this company dominated school district certainly came under corporate purview.

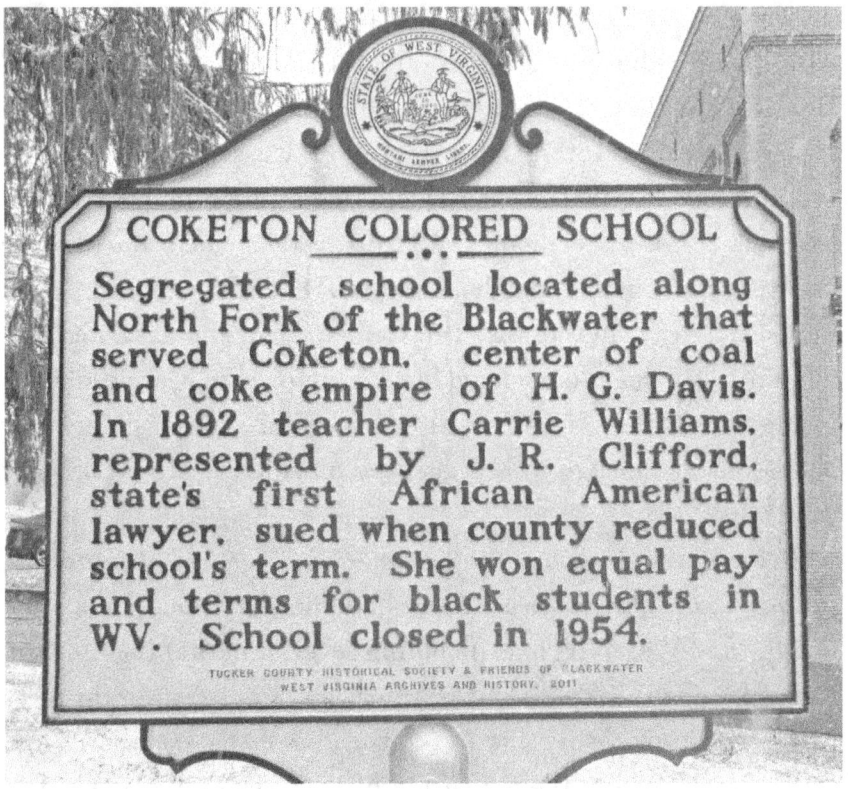

Coketon Colored School, West Virginia Historical Marker
Marker is on Douglas Road / Front Street (County Route 27) half a mile south of Appalachian Highway (West Virginia Route 32)

Despite a vote by the citizens in Tucker County's Fairfax District to fund an eight month school term, the all white Board of Education decided to reduce the school year to five months for African American children in the Coketon Colored School. Clearly, the school board anticipated no resistance to its decision.

As West Virginia historian Connie Park Rice notes, "More than likely board members assumed that African American workers and their families, including Carrie Williams, would be too intimidated to protest the board's new policy. After all, the company that provided the schools and ran the school board also paid their wages and gave them housing, a situation that basically rendered them helpless against the board's new policy."[41] However, the school board soon encountered the quiet, composed and determined strength of Carrie Williams. "She was twenty-six years old; African American, the wife of a coal miner, the mother of two children and pregnant with her third."[42] Rather than being intimidated, Carrie Williams chose to fight this injustice.

Living in a time of profound change in American society and struggling to create a life for themselves, their children and their community, Carrie Williams and her husband Abraham chose a difficult path in challenging the power of the Davis Coal and Coke Company. When presented with her teaching contract that shortened the school year for African American children to five months while retaining an eight-month calendar for the white schools, Carrie Williams chose not to sign. In doing so, she was challenging the powerful coal and railroad empire that was Davis Coal and Coke Company. Later, she testified in court that instead of signing her contract, she "saw counsel." Together with her lawyer, J. R. Clifford, Carrie Williams defeated the Tucker County Board of Education of Fairfax District's order. Her victory not only guaranteed an equal school year for black children as well as equal pay for African American teachers, but also became an essential building block for equal rights in West Virginia. Carrie's unwavering commitment to this cause exemplifies the power of an individual to confront a gross inequity in her life, in the lives of her children and in the lives of her current and future students. Her accomplishment remained a beacon of hope in an era of racially determined second-class citizenship that the *Plessy vs. Ferguson* "separate but equal" doctrine had legitimized.

1. "Early Negro Education In West Virginia," *West Virginia Archives and History* www.wvculture.org/history/africanamericans/woodsoncarter02.html.
2. Rodriguez, Junius P. *The Historical Encyclopedia of World Slavery.* Vol. 1, Santa Barbara, Calif., ABC-CLIO, 1997. p. 42.
3. "A West Virginia Timeline." jeff560.tripod.com/wv-hist.html.
4. Rodriguez, Junius P. *The Historical Encyclopedia of World Slavery.* Vol. 1, Santa Barbara, Calif., ABC-CLIO, 1997. p.42.
5. *Transcript of Interview with Ancella Bickley, June 21, 1992, for the Film "West Virginia."* www.wvculture.org/history/wvmemory/filmtranscripts/wvbickley.html. p.10.
6. "A West Virginia Timeline." jeff560.tripod.com/wv-hist.html.
7. Woodson, C. G. "Early Negro Education in West Virginia." *The Journal of Negro History*, vol. 7, no. 1, Jan. 1922, p. 26.

8. Engle, Stephen D. "Mountaineer Reconstruction: Blacks in the Political Reconstruction of West Virginia." *The Journal of Negro History*, vol. 78, no. 3, 1993, p. 146.
9. Rice, Connie Park. "'Don't Flinch nor Yield an Inch': J. R. Clifford and the Struggle for Equal Rights in West Virginia." *West Virginia History: A Journal of Regional Studies*, vol. 1, no. 2, 2008, p. 49.
10. Bickley, Ancella R. "African-American Education." *West Virginia Encyclopedia*, www.wvencyclopedia.org/articles/26.
11. *Transcript of Interview with Ancella Bickley, June 21, 1992, for the Film "West Virginia."* www.wvculture.org/history/wvmemory/filmtranscripts/wvbickley.html p. 12.
12. Woodson, C. G. "Early Negro Education in West Virginia." *The Journal of Negro History*, vol. 7, no. 1, Jan. 1922, p. 25.
13. Engle, Stephen D. "Mountaineer Reconstruction: Blacks in the Political Reconstruction of West Virginia." *The Journal of Negro History*, vol. 78, no. 3, 1993, p. 146.
14. Ibid.
15. Ibid.
16. Lewis, Ronald. "Black Education in West Virginia in the Segregation Era." *The Pioneer Press - Niagara Centennial Edition*, vol. 125, no. 1, 12 Aug. 2006. p. 5.
17. Ibid.
18. Rice, Connie Park. "'Don't Flinch nor Yield an Inch': J. R. Clifford and the Struggle for Equal Rights in West Virginia." *West Virginia History: A Journal of Regional Studies*, vol. 1, no. 2, 2008, p. 50.

19. Ibid., pp. 50-51.
20. "African-American Population of Present-day West Virginia Counties in 1860 in West Virginia." *West Virginia Archives & History*, www.wvculture.org/history/archives/blacks/timeline.html.
21. "West Virginia Population by Race." *West Virginia Archives & History*, www.wvculture.org/history/archives/teacherresouces/censuspopulationnrace.html.
22. Bickley, Ancella R. "African-American Education." *West Virginia Encyclopedia*, www.wvencyclopedia.org/articles/26.
23. Lewis, Ronald. "Black Education in West Virginia in the Segregation Era." *The Pioneer Press - Niagara Centennial Edition*, vol. 125, no. 1, 12 Aug. 2006. p. 5.
24. Bickley, Ancella R. "African-American Education." *West Virginia Encyclopedia*, www.wvencyclopedia.org/articles/26.
25. Lewis, Ronald. "Black Education in West Virginia in the Segregation Era." *The Pioneer Press - Niagara Centennial Edition*, vol. 125, no. 1, 12 Aug. 2006. p. 5.
26. Armada, Maria. "Doris Green's Memories of Coketon Colored School." *The Pioneer Press - Niagara Centennial Edition*, vol. 125, no. 1, 12 Aug. 2006. p.4.
27. Ibid.
28. Lewis, Ronald. "Black Education in West Virginia in the Segregation Era." *The Pioneer Press - Niagara Centennial Edition*, vol. 125, no. 1, 12 Aug. 2006. p. 5.
29. Ibid.

30. Woodson, C. G. "Early Negro Education in West Virginia." *The Journal of Negro History*, vol. 7, no. 1, Jan. 1922, p.26.
31. *Friends of Blackwater*, Newsletter Oct. 2014, p.4. www.saveblackwater.org/documents/October2014forweb.pdf.
32. *Transcript of Interview with Ancella Bickley, June 21, 1992, for the Film "West Virginia."* www.wvculture.org/history/wvmemory/filmtranscripts/wvbickley.html p.7.
33. Siebert, Wilbur H. "Light on the Underground Railroad." *The American Historical Review*, vol. 1, no. 3, 1896, p. 457.
34. Ibid. pp. 459-460.
35. *African Americans in Antebellum Ohio*. Black, White and Beyond - An Interactive History, learn.uakron.edu/beyond/africanAm_antebellum.htm.
36. Ibid.
37. City of Chillicothe, www.chillicothe.com/history.html.
38. *Friends of Blackwater*, Newsletter Oct. 2014, www.saveblackwater.org/documents/October2014forweb.pdf.
39. Rice, Connie Park. "'Don't Flinch nor Yield an Inch': J. R. Clifford and the Struggle for Equal Rights in West Virginia." *West Virginia History: A Journal of Regional Studies*, vol. 1, no. 2, 2008, pp. 51-52.
40. Ibid., p. 51.
41. Ibid., p. 52.
42. Ibid., p. 51.

CHAPTER SIX

Civil Rights Advocate and Attorney

As African Americans struggled to secure legal, educational and economic opportunities in the post Civil War period, the acute shortage of black lawyers presented dramatic challenges. With the effective end of Radical Reconstruction in the Compromise of 1877, the Republican Party now focused its energy on economic development. The once self proclaimed protector of the rights of the freedmen, the Republican Party of the Reconstruction era, gave way to a new party whose primary concern was anchored in the politics of big business in the burgeoning industrial growth of the nation. No longer courting the black vote, Republicans now sought economic opportunities at the expense of the African Americans that they had once pledged to support.[1]

Consequently, African Americans were left in a precarious position in the South where nearly ninety percent of the black population lived. Even during Radical Reconstruction, the freedmen were frequently victimized by disenfranchised whites who used violence as a means of intimidation. The birth of the Klu Klux Klan, "a secret terrorist organization that operated outside of the law... The Klan's strength increased in direct proportion to southern black citizens' assertion of their rights... A tortured corpse was a grim warning to an aspiring citizen who might be considering starting his own farm or running for office."[2] With the end of Radical Reconstruction came the re-enfranchisement of former Confederates, who, along with newcomers from northern states in pursuit of economic gain, pursued a systematic policy of second-class citizenship for African Americans.

Despite the efforts of black leaders such as Hiram Revels and Blanche Bruce, both United States Senators from Mississippi, and the fifteen African American men in the U.S. House of Representatives during Reconstruction, by 1890 little remained of the Radical Republican well intended safeguarding of the rights of the freedmen. At the same time, African Americans found themselves with relatively little legal representation. Although white lawyers did represent black clients, African Americans experienced the critical need for black attorneys to represent their interests in an era increasingly characterized by a racially stratified society sanctioned by law.

As the Compromise of 1877 formally ended Reconstruction, over time the South enacted Jim Crow laws that disenfranchised African Americans and legalized segregation in all aspects of life. Prior to this, the common laws among the newly reconstructed southern states had prohibited racial intermarriage and integrated schools. In addition, West Virginia's 1872 revised constitution included these two provisions. However, in 1883, when the Supreme Court declared Charles Sumner's Civil Rights Act of 1875 unconstitutional, a new era was launched. The use of grandfather clauses, poll taxes and literacy tests to disenfranchise the black man in the South became just one step in the process of complete racial discrimination.

When the state of Mississippi, free of Radical Republican oversight, revised its constitution in 1890, blacks were officially relegated to second-class citizenship. The newly revised constitution included a suffrage amendment that required a poll tax, disqualification for "criminals," and the ability to read, understand, and interpret the state constitution, consequently eliminating the right to vote for many poor and illiterate blacks.[3] As it tested the political tenor of the time, Mississippi's state constitution also provided a model for other southern states in their policies of de jure segregation. South Carolina followed suit with a similar amendment in 1895, while three years later, Louisiana introduced the grandfather clause that allowed suffrage only to those whose father and grandfather had been allowed to vote as of January 1, 1867.[4]

J. R. Clifford adamantly opposed the Louisiana law stating, "This editor's (Clifford) grandfather had no rights, but he fought for his, and it is not what his grandfather was then, but what he is now."[5] However, as African American disenfranchisement became the established standard, southern states soon enacted new laws requiring segregation in all aspects of public life, including railroad cars, hotels, restaurants, theaters, and streetcars.[6] Although attempts were made in West Virginia to disenfranchise African American men and to segregate West

Virginians, black leaders worked effectively to block these efforts. However, de facto segregation became the norm.[7]

As the policy of segregation became entrenched, African Americans sought relief in the courts. While Carrie Williams successfully achieved legal redress in her lawsuit against the Tucker County Board of Education in West Virginia, others did not experience such a positive outcome. In 1890, Louisiana passed the Separate Car Act requiring segregated railway cars within the state. Knowing that the East Louisiana Railway in New Orleans only provided first class cars for whites while blacks were relegated to third class cars, African American Homer Plessy purchased a first class ticket. When Plessy refused to leave his seat in the "white" car, he was arrested and fined. Backed by a Committee of Citizens composed of black professionals, Plessy unsuccessfully challenged the constitutionality of the law in this test case. In 1896, the Supreme Court's decision in *Plessy vs. Ferguson* established the doctrine of "separate but equal," legalizing segregated facilities for African Americans, and in effect, sanctioning white supremacy.

This doctrine would not be overturned for fifty-eight years until the Supreme Court ruled in favor of Linda Brown, a third grader, whose parents had sued the Board of Education of Topeka, Kansas for its refusal to admit her to the all white school, Sumner Elementary, located seven blocks from her home. Attending the black school, Monroe Elementary, required that the third grader walk six blocks to a bus stop and then travel the remaining distance of one mile on the school bus. Ironically, the all white school was named for Charles Sumner, the Radical Republican senator from Massachusetts who had spent his public life advocating for the rights of African Americans.

In an unanimous decision written by Chief Justice Earl Warren, the Supreme Court declared that, "in the field of public education, the doctrine of 'separate but equal' has no place. Separate educational facilities are inherently unequal..." The Court further stated that the "separate but equal" doctrine violated the equal protection of the law clause of the 14th Amendment.[8] Again, historical irony prevails. During Reconstruction, the ratification of the 14th Amendment was a requirement for a former Confederate state to reenter the Union and its two essential stipulations, the due process clause and the equal protection clause, were designed to protect the rights of citizens under state jurisdiction. A further irony is that the 14th Amendment's equal protection clause was the argument that J. R. Clifford used in his battle to achieve fair educational standards for black children in West Virginia. Coincidentally, earlier in his career, Clifford had been a teacher and principal of the Sumner School in Martinsburg, another educational institution named for the senator.

At the same time that the freedmen found themselves disenfranchised, they were caught in the web of sharecropping as they struggled to achieve an economic foothold in the South. In this economic system, the freedmen as tenant farmers or sharecroppers in effect performed the work of the former slaves on land that they rented. Intrinsic to sharecropping was the lien system where exorbitant interest rates or liens were placed on loans to acquire the necessary equipment and supplies. These fees along with the landowner's rent left African Americas locked in a cycle of poverty with the status of a peon. For most African Americans, the financial burden of any form of advanced education was prohibitive. Truly, life for African Americans in this period was a combination of political disenfranchisement and economic marginalization.

The need for African American lawyers was never greater than in the post Civil War period that was quite literally and legally defined by a racially divided society. In their quest for admission to the bar, black attorneys faced astounding obstacles. Once admitted, they were often met with such virulent racism and discrimination that black lawyers were "assaulted, run out of town, or even killed" for practicing in the South.[9] It was not uncommon for African American lawyers to be referred to as "niggers" by opposing counsel and even judges. By choosing law as a career, African Americans lawyers were not only attorneys, but also social engineers, fostering societal change and aiding in the struggle for equality, consciously or unconsciously, as they practiced law despite intense prejudice and discrimination.[10]

Given the inequities that so many blacks encountered in the pursuit of any form of higher education, the shortage of African American lawyers is not surprising. For those pursuing a career in law, essentially two paths existed: reading the law which meant, in effect, apprenticing with a practicing attorney; or attending a law school. Before the 1890s, most aspiring students "read" law under the supervision of an experienced attorney. However, the legal profession was moving to more formal training in a law school setting. Both of these options presented obstacles for blacks. All too often, it was difficult for an African American to find an attorney, usually a white lawyer, willing to mentor that student in his office. Attending a law school also presented difficulties since an applicant needed money for tuition, and by the early twentieth century, an undergraduate degree.[11]

Following Reconstruction, most African Americans seeking law as a career followed the apprenticeship method. However, as more black law schools opened, increasingly African Americans followed this legal path. In 1869, Howard Law School provided critically needed legal education when it became the first law school in the nation to establish an admissions policy that did not discriminate on the basis of race or gender. Between 1872 and 1904, in addition to the African American male graduates, eight black women and seven white women graduated from Howard Law School.[12] Among the Howard Law graduates were Thomas Gillis Nutter and Emory Rankin Carter both of whom became prominent lawyers in West Virginia.[13] Other black law schools opened only to close quickly: Lincoln University Law School, Shaw University Law School and Central Tennessee opened and closed between 1870 and 1921 due to lack of funding, resources and even students. Some aspiring black men attended law schools in the North through the sponsorship of a white philanthropist. For example, Mark Twain financed the legal education of Warner T. McGuinn at Yale and Silas N. Strawn, a former president of the American Bar Association, assisted Euclid Taylor at a law school in Chicago.[14]

Passing the bar also presented racial hurdles. During this time period, applicants had oral examinations and interviews. Often, race played a pernicious role as seen in the comment of one of the examiners of James Weldon Johnson, the first black man admitted to the Florida bar. In response to an examiner's statement, "He's passed a good examination," Johnson heard another examiner's reply, "Well, I can't forget he's a nigger and I'll be damned if I stay here and see him admitted."[15] Despite these difficulties, African Americans did persist in their legal studies.

However, the shortage of lawyers continued. In 1887, there were only 440 African American lawyers in the nation, the majority of whom practiced in the North.[16] Looking at the South, lawyers were scarce: in 1900, Mississippi had twenty-four black lawyers and South Carolina had twenty-nine. These numbers declined steadily until by 1920, both states had a combined total of fourteen black lawyers.[17] Consequently, black clients experienced great difficulty in engaging African American lawyers. While white attorneys represented black clients, in a courtroom, African Americans usually were confronted with an all white jury that questioned the validity of black testimony.

The role of the black lawyer as social engineer was inextricably woven into the social and racial mores of the times. Whether or not black lawyers sought the mantle of crusader for greater equality between the races, this role was an inevitable result of admission to the bar. Consequently, as legal historian Paul Finkelman observes, "Their (black lawyers) very presence in courtrooms altered the way whites and blacks viewed race relations."[18] Not only did black lawyers demonstrate black accomplishment, but also they "undermined the pervasive psychology of racism."[19] By providing representation to African Americans, black lawyers could not help but to challenge the existing relegation of racially defined second-class citizenship sanctioned by law.

When Carrie Williams received her teaching contract that had shortened the "colored" school term to five months while maintaining an eight-month term for white students, she chose to fight this injustice. However, at this time, there were only fourteen African American lawyers in the entire state of West Virginia. Fortunately for her own children and the children of the Coketon Colored School, J. R. Clifford accepted this case.

The life of John Robert Clifford unfolded in the midst of great change in the United States. Not only was West Virginia evolving as a new state striving to establish its identity in the midst of the Civil War and its aftermath, but also the nation itself struggled to ensure that all citizens experience the rights of American democracy. Although Radical Reconstruction attempted to guarantee civil rights to African Americans, in its aftermath, the nation continued to grapple with the legacy of slavery and the relegation of blacks to second-class citizenship. As W.E.B. Du Bois aptly assessed, "For the American Negro, the last decade of the nineteenth and the first part of the twentieth centuries were more critical than the Reconstruction years of 1868 to 1876."[20] It is within this context that Clifford consistently challenged the prevalent societal norms in pursuit of equal justice for African Americans.

To trace the life of John Robert Clifford is to embark upon a journey, a particularly American journey, rooted in the first great watershed of American history, the Civil War. From his childhood working on his parent's farm near Moorefield, Virginia (later West Virginia) to his initial education in Chicago to his rise to the rank of corporal in the Union Army, J. R. Clifford sought to define himself in the new world that the Civil War engendered for African Americans. His work as an educator and as the editor of the *Pioneer Press* helped to prepare him for his greatest role as an attorney championing equal rights for African Americans. Intrinsic to the underlying theme of his life's work is his belief in the dual power of education and the law as the great conduit of success for whites and blacks alike.

John Robert Clifford
Image Source: Pioneer Press, JR Clifford Project

John Robert Clifford was born in Hardy (present day Grant County) County at Williamsport near Moorefield, Virginia, in September of 1848. His parents, Isaac and Mary Satilpa Clifford, as well as their ancestors, were free blacks as far back as they can be traced in western Virginia. Indeed, Hardy County was the only county in Virginia that had more free people of color than slaves.[21] The Virginia of Clifford's childhood was not the Virginia of the antebellum South. The rugged mountains of what would become the state of West Virginia did not lend itself to the peculiar institution. As Clifford's grandson Paul Ingram Clifford notes, "In Appalachian America, the races maintain a sort of social contact. White and Black men work side by side, visit each other in their homes and often attend the same church with delight to the Word spoken by either a colored or White preacher."[22] However, education for black children was non-existent. Not only did Virginia law forbid teaching African American children to read and write, the Virginia Code of 1860 further prohibited free blacks "who left the state, even for an education, from returning."[23]

Believing strongly in the necessity of education for their son, and most likely, desiring to remove him from the armed conflict, the Cliffords sent young J. R. to Chicago where he lived with a family friend, a young white man John J. Healy and his wife Nellie. Here, living among the Healy family and attending an integrated school not only encouraged young J. R. to strive for improvement, but also reinforced his belief in equality among the races.[24] Although Healy was only five years older than Clifford, he clearly regarded him as a father figure, describing him as a "loving tender father in goodness... and that if our (Clifford's) life amounts to anything, the credit is placed to Captain John J.

Healy."[25] This friendship of more than forty-six years between a white Irishman from the city of Chicago and an African American man from rural Hardy County models the blessings of a truly integrated society.[26] Years later, J. R. Clifford spoke of a joyous return to Chicago as he happily reunited with his former classmates and teacher.

> Our early life was spent in the schools of Chicago,... about ten years later, we returned to Chicago and going to the Appellate Court found our class and seat mate, Mr. Frank Lane, head clerk over more than a hundred clerks. We embraced each other... he got his buggy and took us all over all of our prank grounds and O! what a time we had that day: One of the old teachers threw her arms around us and many of the then boys were then men in various kinds of business and all greeted us and Mrs. Curtain, one of the noblest and sweetest women Chicago ever owned... greeted us as a mother would her long gone and returned son.[27]

For Clifford, these early societal and educational experiences solidified his belief that the races, black and white together, could truly forge a fair and equitable society, a goal that he would actively pursue throughout his life.

While attending school in Chicago, Clifford experienced an urban environment for the first time. As the midwestern city that Senator Stephen Douglas envisioned as the eastern terminus of the transcontinental railroad built after the Civil War, Chicago was already alive with the activity of a thriving metropolis on the verge of the industrial age, a far cry from the mountains of West Virginia. Chicago also became the adopted home of Mother Mary Jones, a woman once proclaimed by an incensed West Virginia U.S. District Attorney to be the most dangerous woman in

America for her work in galvanizing striking coal miners in the unionization process. Here, a young Joseph Hoke also traveled from Virginia (later West Virginia) on his way to Rock River Seminary just one hundred and nine miles west of Chicago. And Illinois would become the eventual home of Carrie Williams long after the victory of *Williams vs. Tucker County Board of Education of Fairfax District.* It was here in March of 1865 that a young sixteen-year old J. R. Clifford, accompanied by now Captain John J. Healy of the 23rd Regiment of the Illinois Volunteers known as Mulligan's Irish Brigade, enlisted in the Union Army as a member of the U.S. Colored Troops.[28]

For young J. R. Clifford, the inspiring words of Frederick Douglass who urged African American men to enlist in the Union army were a defining call that foreshadowed not only his military service, but also his future battles in and out of the courtroom. "Men of Color, to Arms!... Once let the black man get upon his person the brass letters 'U.S.,' let him get an eagle on his button, and a musket on his shoulder and bullets in his pocket, and there is no power on earth that can deny that he has earned the right to citizenship."[29] Assigned to Company F, 13th Kentucky Regiment of Heavy Artillery, headquartered at Camp Nelson, Kentucky, Clifford served until November of 1865, having reached the rank of Corporal. Company F consisted of African American men from Illinois, Michigan and Kentucky with Sergeant Major Francis A. Adams as the highest-ranking African American in the regiment.[30]

As a young soldier training at Camp Nelson, Clifford must have been filled with awed respect and pride when he saw thousands of black soldiers ready for battle. At the same time, he must have witnessed the severe conditions that existed for the families of African American soldiers as the Civil War ensued. Originally established as a supply depot for Union invasions into Tennessee, Camp Nelson soon proved to be inadequate for this task and General Ulysses Grant wanted to abandon it. However, General William Tecumseh Sherman advised diminishing its role as a supply depot and Camp Nelson subsequently became the third largest recruiting, mustering and training center for African American troops. Other U.S. Colored Troops trained at larger facilities in Boston and New Orleans[31] as well as at smaller camps in Philadelphia, Indianapolis and Arlington County, Virginia, among others. Troops from Camp Nelson participated in the southwestern Virginia campaigns, the siege of Petersburg, Virginia, and the pursuit of the Army of Northern Virginia to Appomattox Courthouse as well as performing garrison duty throughout Kentucky.[32]

United States Colored Troops, at Fort Lincoln, District of Columbia
Library of Congress

In addition, Camp Nelson was a contraband or refugee camp for family members of colored troop recruits. Nearly 10,000 African Americans were emancipated from slavery in exchange for service in the Union army, many bringing their families with them. At one point, 3,060 refugees lived at Camp Nelson, cared for by missionaries who along with army personnel struggled to provide adequate facilities.[33] U.S. Army Captain Theron Hall and the Reverend John G. Fee of the American Missionary Association provided cottages, dormitories, a hospital and a school in addition to a dining room and laundry for over three thousand people.[34] At one point, because Camp Nelson was not a legal refugee site, Union soldiers forced two hundred women and children from the camp. Refugees suffered one hundred and two deaths due to severe weather until they were readmitted. Overall, nearly three thousand refugees died at Camp Nelson as a result of infectious diseases. Subsequent federal legislation emancipated family members of the U.S. Colored Troops and provided a formal program to care for and educate refugees.[35] At the conclusion of the war, Camp Nelson was a center for giving former slaves emancipation papers, earning the camp's title of "Cradle of Freedom."

As difficult as life was for so many at Camp Nelson, one African American soldier poignantly wrote, "I can stand this, said I. This is better than slavery, though I do march in line at the tap of a drum. I felt freedom in my bones, and when I saw the American eagle with outspread wings, upon the American flag, with the motto E Pluribus Unum, the thought came to me, 'Give me liberty or give me death.' Then all fear banished."[36] Sergeant William A. Warfield of the 119th United States Colored Troops concurred, as he joined in the Fourth of July celebration at Camp

Nelson, stating, "To see so many thousands, who a year ago were slaves, congregate in the heart of a slave state and celebrate the day sacred to the cause of freedom, 'with none to molest or make afraid', was a grand spectacle."[37]

It is difficult to gauge the breadth of what J. R. Clifford experienced during his training at Camp Nelson and in his service as an artillery soldier in the Civil War where he served in Kentucky, Tennessee and eastern Virginia under General Ulysses S. Grant.[38] What does emerge in this character portrait of a teenage boy moving into manhood are the salient traits that will guide his life: a commitment to hard work, an understanding of the necessity of education and the perseverance to actualize his goals, all fueled by J. R. Clifford's empathy for his fellow man, especially the newly freedmen and their families in their struggles for full citizenship. After the Civil War, Clifford remained in Chicago with the Healy family until he graduated from Chicago High School. Working briefly as a barber, he then spent time with his uncle in Zeno, Muskingum County, Ohio, where he received a diploma from a writing school conducted by Professor D. A. White before conducting his own writing school for nearly one hundred students in Wheeling, West Virginia and later in Martin's Ferry, Ohio.[39]

In 1873, Clifford entered Storer Normal College in Harper's Ferry, West Virginia. After graduating in 1876, Clifford taught at the Sumner School in Martinsburg where he was later promoted to the position of principal. In December of 1876, he married Mary Franklin, a native of Harper's Ferry and fellow graduate of Storer, in a ceremony performed by the Reverend Nathan Brackett, the founder and president of Storer College. J.R. and Mary Clifford had eleven children, several of whom died before reaching adulthood.[40] Although remaining a loyal alumnus, later as editor of the *Pioneer Press*, Clifford criticized the all white administration of Storer College, believing that African Americans should have a greater role in the mission of this historic institution.

1882 was a pivotal year in the life of J. R. Clifford. In the early 1880s, he became a member of the Knights of Wise Men, an African American fraternal organization whose national membership included Henry McNeal Turner, John Roy Lynch and John Wesley Cromwell.[41] Not only did this organization offer him the opportunity to engage with other emerging black leaders, but it also provided Clifford a broader forum for his views. His speech at the 1882 national meeting in Atlanta, Georgia, cast him as a crucial voice in advocating equal rights for blacks in the changing South of the post Reconstruction period.

This move into a national forum coalesced with his founding of the *Pioneer Press* in 1882. As the first African American newspaper in West Virginia, the *Pioneer Press* found readers across the country as it attempted to address the "moral, religious and financial needs," not just for African American subscribers, but all of humanity, on a weekly basis.[42] Also publicized as a Republican newspaper, Clifford used the *Pioneer Press* as a vehicle to examine the changing Republican policies in the post Reconstruction era. However, his analysis frequently contributed to what historian Connie Park Rice describes as igniting "both racial and class conflict that resulted in attacks on his paper... as well as physical violence against his person."[43]

Clifford's outspoken criticism of local and state Republican politicians, both black and white, often precipitated clashes with the political establishment that negatively impacted Clifford's newspaper, and by 1890, he had lost all of his associate editors in the state. However, since few issues remain from this decade, it is unclear why these associate editors left the *Pioneer Press*. This separation could have resulted from other commitments, a mutual decision between Clifford and the associate editors or a choice by the editors to align themselves with the Republican Party boss, Stephen B. Elkins, who promised benefits to loyal black leaders.[44] At this time, Clifford, having passed the West Virginia bar in 1887, was also in the midst of establishing his legal practice.

Consequently, by 1890, Clifford named John W. Cromwell co-editor of the *Pioneer Press* for the first few years of the decade.[45] Clifford had originally met Cromwell, the former editor of the *Washington (D.C.) People's Advocate,* at the 1882 national meeting of the Knights of Wise Men in Atlanta. The *Pioneer Press* remained one of the most respected black newspapers in the nation until its closing by the federal government due to Clifford's editorial criticisms of the United States' involvement in World War I. At the time of its demise, it was the longest running black newspaper in the country.[46]

Clifford's struggle for social justice that found such eloquent expression in his work as a newspaper editor was fueled by an earlier event in his life. In August of 1874, the twenty-five year old college student witnessed an event that would have a profound effect on his life: the lynching of a young black man named James Tallifero in nearby Martinsburg. Tallifero's murder sparked a chain of events that placed Clifford in direct conflict with local Republican leaders and led to a lifelong commitment to fighting for equal rights.[47] Clifford later fought the appointment of Republican George F. Evans as Postmaster of Martinsburg because of his involvement in the Tallifero lynching, urging blacks to petition the United States Senate Committee not to approve Evans as Postmaster of Martinsburg. By supporting the Democratic candidate J. Nelson Wisner, the white lawyer with whom Clifford had studied law, he angered local Republican leaders.

Later in the 1892 election for representative of Jefferson County to the state legislature, Clifford experienced the pernicious effect of racial slurs and misrepresentations, this time, compliments of the Democratic Party. Supporting the Republican candidate, Hamilton Hatter, a black instructor at Storer College, Clifford witnessed the Democratic Party's skillful appeal to white fears of the consequences of sending Hatter to Charleston. Democrats disseminated "lithographs portraying an integrated schoolroom under the instruction of a 'burly Negro.'... In the poster, the teacher brutally chastised a beautiful white girl as Negro pupils laughed with ghoulish glee." Not only did the Democrats defeat Hatter, but also they solidified Democratic control of the state government.[48]

Clifford's problematic political associations, especially with the Republican Party, continued. Although elected by the West Virginia State Republican Convention as a delegate-at-large to the national Republican Convention in Chicago, Clifford's opponents effectively robbed him of this status by changing votes and eliminating him.[49] Despite their prior friendship and Clifford's political support,[50] leading this challenge was W. H. H. Flick, a white lawyer who had refused to have Clifford study law with him, giving the reason for his refusal as "for want of time and on the same day in my (Clifford's) presence offered to take a white student."[51]

Clifford then described the opposition to him as a delegate by quoting William H. Riggs, chairman of the Republican County Executive Committee, "The idea of a nigger taking part in a white man's fight" as well as another Republican member stating, "No d--n nigger will go to Chicago as a delegate from this State."[52] Not only was Clifford robbed of his position as a delegate, but also he was overlooked as an alternate delegate, a position usually afforded to African Americans. Flick denied his involvement in robbing Clifford of his delegate status, but Clifford proclaimed, "They tried their level best to paralyze me politically, but they have given me new vitality."[53] Subsequently, Republican Party leaders unsuccessfully attempted to have Clifford fired from the Sumner School in Martinsburg. Eventually, in May of 1886, Clifford resigned as principal to devote his energies to the *Pioneer Press* and preparation for the bar examination.

Assessing his political involvement in West Virginia, Clifford wrote in the *Pioneer Press* in 1886, "That I have been a Republican fanatic in this State for the past 16 years, toiling irksomely to the detriment of time, my pocket-book, my past position and family and that damns have been my remuneration... That there are genuine Republicans in this State, we have no doubt, and were they at the head of affairs our past fealty to the party would be the same today; but it is not so..."[54] As West Virginia University historian Connie Park Rice observes, "a long history of animosity existed between Clifford and local Republican leaders who often criticized Clifford's failure 'to know his place'..."[55] However, Clifford remained steadfast in his opposition to what he regarded as black accommodation to white Republican politics in the post Reconstruction era.

While Clifford's outspoken criticism of Republican politics put him in a somewhat marginalized position among local Republicans, it was his legal role that profoundly impacted the lives of black Americans in West Virginia. As the first African American admitted to the bar, Clifford effectively challenged the stereotype of the black male in a precarious time in which the dominant white society had successfully disenfranchised many African Americans and had legalized a racially stratified society. Clifford's 1887 admission to the bar was a challenge in itself, evoking deeply held animosity.[56] Clifford clearly relished his legal role as social engineer. As historian Paul Finkelman has noted, black attorneys threatened the psychology of racism. "Every time a black lawyer won a case against a white lawyer or represented a white client, he or she exposed the fraud of white supremacy."[57] In and out of the courtroom, Clifford represented the solid accomplishment of the self-made man who challenged racism on multiple levels. At the same time, intrinsic to Clifford's life view was the belief in what all people, black and white, together could achieve in the pursuit of social justice protected by law.

In 1896, J. R. Clifford became involved in quite literally a legal "battle." Just a few months earlier, Booker T. Washington, an African American who had grown up in West Virginia, proclaimed the Atlanta Compromise that advocated black accommodation, advising "blacks to remain in the South and whites to look to their loyal black population as a labor force, while assuring his predominantly white audience at the Cotton States and International Exposition that in all things purely social we can be as separate as the fingers."[58] For Clifford, the

1895 Atlanta Compromise was an anathema that only intensified his battle for equal rights for African Americans.

In direct contrast to Booker T. Washington's acceptance of second-class citizenship, Clifford demanded the seating of black jurors in the voir dire process in a Berkeley courtroom. Despite the 1879 West Virginia Supreme Court decision in *Strauder vs. West Virginia* that gave blacks in West Virginia the right to serve as jurors, most counties refused to allow it.[59] However, Clifford tenaciously persisted, insisting that blacks be empaneled as jurors. Incensed at his efforts, the Prosecuting Attorney of Berkeley County, U.S.G. Pitzer struck Clifford with deadly weights "three times until his blood ran in his shoes."[60] While Clifford prevailed in seating African American jurors, he ultimately lost the case. Although no record of assault charges is to be found,[61] Clifford bided his time until the fall of 1898 when Pizter ran as the Republican candidate for Congress. Declaring himself an independent candidate for the same seat, Clifford campaigned wearing his bloody shirt. Neither Clifford nor Pitzer won the election which went to Henry S. Cushwa, the Democratic candidate who defeated Pitzer by more than 1,300 votes, "just as Clifford intended... Clifford had his justice... and he kept the bloody shirt as a souvenir."[62]

Deeply troubled by the continuing codification of second-class citizenship for blacks, Clifford steadfastly championed the due process and equal protection of the law clauses of the 14th Amendment as the guarantor of the rights of all citizens. While more than fifty years ahead of his time, he adamantly invoked these vitally important clauses in two of his greatest legal achievements, both involving discrimination in the field of education. Firmly believing that segregated schools were by their nature inherently inferior for blacks, Clifford made inroads in a system that was codified by the state's 1872 revised constitution. While the 1866 West Virginia state legislature had passed a law to create black public schools, the law's intent to segregate black and white students remained unclear until the state revised its constitution in 1872 to affirm that blacks and whites could not be taught in the same schools.[63] Although unable to end segregated schools, Clifford's legal efforts resulted in crucial gains for African Americans in West Virginia. In both *Martin vs. Morgan County Board of Education* and *Williams vs. Tucker County Board of Education of Fairfax District*, Clifford achieved significant legal success for the black children of West Virginia.

In 1893, J. R. Clifford brought the first legal challenge of the segregated school system in West Virginia on behalf of African American Thomas Martin, a well-respected member of his Paw Paw, Morgan County community where he was a founder and trustee of the Mt. Olive Church and a member of both the Odd Fellows and the Masons. Martin was a self-educated farmer and a Civil War veteran who had advanced to the rank of sergeant in the Union Army.[64] Naturally, education for his five children was a priority. However, since the Martins were the only African Americans in the area, no "colored" school existed. Consequently, on January 23, 1893, Thomas and Louisiann Martin sent their five children to the nearby Camp Hill School where the teacher, Mr. M. A. Vanorsdale, refused to admit Samuel, Phillip, Fenton, Rachel and Nancy on racial grounds.[65]

On March 23, 1893, Clifford filed a petition and application for a writ of mandamus for Thomas Martin against the Board of Education and Trustees of Cacapon District, Sub-District No.4 of Morgan County.[66] For J. R. Clifford who had come to view segregated education as marking African Americans with "a badge of inferiority,"[67] the Martin case offered the legal opportunity to challenge the constitutionality of the West Virginia state law. Once in court, Clifford encountered a former legal opponent, W. H. H. Flick, who represented the Morgan County Board of Education. Arguing the necessity of admitting black children to an all white school where districts failed to provide schools for African American children, Clifford sought to test the West Virginia segregated school system by demonstrating that it violated both the due process and the equal protection of the law clauses of the 14th Amendment. However, Judge E. Boyd Faulkner, a descendant of an influential antebellum family and a former captain in the Confederate Army disagreed.[68] Holding that "mixed schools" would violate the West Virginia state constitution and "for other reasons which it is unnecessary to mention," Judge Faulkner ignored Clifford's 14th Amendment argument saying that its application would violate the state constitution.[69]

Later, in September of 1896, Clifford became the first African American lawyer to appear before the West Virginia Supreme Court of Appeals where he sought to overturn the *Martin vs. Morgan County Board of Education* lower court's ruling. Clifford's eloquent argument was again rooted in the original intent of the due process and equal protection clauses of the 14th Amendment. Recognizing that Article XII, Section 8, of the West Virginia Constitution of 1872 established segregated schools for white and black students, he argued that when a school board failed to provide equal facilities for white and African American children such a law establishing segregated schools "is contrary to the 14th Amendment and is void." Furthermore, Clifford maintained that the Martin children should be admitted to the white school.[70] In his view, court enforcement of the true purpose of the 14th Amendment would protect civil rights for all Americans. However, Clifford's appeal was fifty-eight years premature. It would not be until the United States Supreme Court's unanimous ruling in the *Brown vs. the Board of Education of Topeka, Kansas,* that segregated education would be deemed "inherently unequal" and in violation of the 14th Amendment's equal protection clause for all citizens. However, in an era in which the United States Supreme Court had recently sanctioned the "separate but equal" doctrine in *Plessy vs. Ferguson*, Clifford's arguments carried little weight.

In the opinion written by Judge Marmaduke Dent, the state's high court asserted that the West Virginia state constitution held dominance over the 14th Amendment of the United States Constitution. Dent further explained, "Such a determination (i.e. to force a white school to admit black children) would be, in effect, permitting the neglect of the legislature or board of education to abrogate the state Constitution, while it is the paramount duty of this Court to see that they obey it." As Dent contended, "Social equality cannot be enforced by law."[71] Dent's opinion, particularly his assertion that the West Virginia state constitution superseded the due process and equal protection clauses of the 14th Amendment, is startling to the current mindset. However, Dent's views, for the most part, are reflective of the post Reconstruction period.[72] In contrast, the basis of Clifford's civil rights crusade is more than half a century ahead of its time.

Unfortunately, like the lower court, the West Virginia Supreme Court of Appeals left the Martin family with no access to public education. However, after this costly and highly publicized court case, the Morgan County Board of Education built a school for African Americans. In light of the recent *Plessy* decision, Clifford had no realistic recourse of appeal. Despite the court's opinion, the Martin case remains the first legal attack on segregated public schools in West Virginia and certainly one of the first legal challenges to segregated schools in the South.[73] In the Martin case, Clifford established a legal precedent by invoking the 14th Amendment's admonition that all citizens are entitled to due process and the equal protection of the law, a precedent that twentieth century lawyers later successfully used in the civil rights movement.

In 1898, Clifford achieved his greatest success as a civil rights advocate in the *Williams vs. Tucker County Board of Education of Fairfax District* case. When Carrie Williams, the teacher at the Coketon Colored School, received her contract that shortened the school year for black children to five months while retaining an eight-month calendar for the white children, rather than acquiesce, she engaged J. R. Clifford as her attorney. Upon counsel's advice, Williams did not sign her five-month contract; instead she taught for the eight-month calendar year and then sued the district for the three months owed in unpaid salary. The 1895 trial victory in the Williams case and the subsequent West Virginia Supreme Court of Appeals upholding of the lower court decision is a landmark event in protecting the rights of African American children to an equal school year as well as equal pay for their teachers. (This case is discussed in detail in the following chapter.)

Clifford remained an opponent of continued attempts to codify second-class citizenship in his home state. However, after years of successfully fighting the establishment of Jim Crow segregated railroad cars in West Virginia, Clifford remained "fearful of the situation... With the chasm between white and black in America at its widest point since the Civil War, for the first time he began to question the nation's acceptance of foreign immigrants into American society while refusing to integrate native born black citizens simply due to the color of their skin."[74] Still, Clifford doubted that Jim Crow legislation would be passed in the Mountain State because, as he believed, there were "too many good and liberal minded men in West Virginia" of both parties to allow such injurious legislation to be enacted.[75]

Clifford fought injustice in private ways, too. In 1915, Clifford boycotted the Norfolk and Western Railroad. Although no Jim Crow laws existed in West Virginia, the railroad had segregated facilities between Shepherdstown and Shenandoah Junction near Charles Town in Jefferson County. If sixty-seven year old Clifford had business in Charles Town, he would take the train to Shepherdstown and then walk the five miles to Shenandoah Junction rather than ride in the segregated car.[76] Clifford's objections also found voice in his editorials in the *Pioneer Press*. "The absurdity of a railway company compelling American citizens to ride in stinking parts of cars, where roughs may drink, curse and swear and the finest ladies be subjected thereto, and that in the state of West Virginia. It is and has been done by the Norfolk and Western for years and by allowing it, it has gone a step further and built a 'nigger waiting room' in Shepherdstown and Charles Town."[77] Here his actions and his writings not only targeted social injustice of his time, but also demonstrated the pernicious spread of that injustice when unchecked.

Clifford continued his public life of service not only to African Americans, but also to West Virginia. In addition to his role as a founding member of the Niagara Movement, Clifford, along with William Monroe Trotter and Reverend J. Milton Waldron, formed the National Negro-American Political League (later the National Independent Political League), serving as president from 1911 to 1913.[78] Over his lifetime, he became a 32nd Degree Mason, a lecturer for the Most Worshipful Prince Hall Grand Lodge of West Virginia, and a Past Grand Master of West Virginia. In addition, as a West Virginia state lecturer, he taught summer institutes for African American teachers as well as becoming the state commissioner of the colored department of the New Orleans Exposition. Clifford was also a charter member of the American Negro Academy, advocating the importance of higher education for African Americans as part of the struggle for racial equality. Described as the "dean of black editors," Clifford was the only African American member of the West Virginia State Editorial Association.

In 1933, Clifford died at age eighty-five in his home in Martinsburg. Originally buried at Mt Hope Cemetery, Clifford was later reinterred at Arlington National Cemetery in 1954 in recognition of his service during the Civil War. His simple tombstone reads: John Clifford, CPL, Co F, 13 US CLD, HV ARTY, Sept 15 1847 (should be 1848) Oct 6 1933.[79] While Clifford prided himself on his Civil War service, his admirers would concur with Du Bois' assessment that "his exploits as a fighter for Negro rights read like a romance,"[80] a true knight in search of the Holy Grail of social justice for African Americans. In Du Bois' estimation, Clifford was truly one of the "talented tenth," an exceptional man who helped to save his race. As a soldier, a teacher, a principal, an editor and an attorney, J. R. Clifford embodied the nobility of cause with an unwavering commitment to social justice. His prophetic vision of the importance of the equal protection of the law clause of the 14th Amendment still remains the unwavering standard for American civil rights.

Perhaps Clifford's own words are his most fitting epitaph. "When a boy I was a farmer, then a waiter, next a barber, then a teacher, next an editor and last a lawyer and the first to be admitted to practice in my state. I used them all as a means to the final end."[81] That end was a lifelong pursuit of social justice in service to his fellow humanity.

1. Rice, Connie Park. "'Don't Flinch nor Yield an Inch': J. R. Clifford and the Struggle for Equal Rights in West Virginia." *West Virginia History: A Journal of Regional Studies*, vol. 1, no. 2, 2008, p. 47.
2. Blum, John M. *The National Experience: A History of the United States.* 8th ed., San Diego, New York, Chicago, Atlanta, Washington D.C., London, Sydney, and Toronto, Cengage Learning, January 2, 1993. p. 415.
3. Rice, Connie Park. "'Don't Flinch nor Yield an Inch': J. R. Clifford and the Struggle for Equal Rights in West Virginia." *West Virginia History: A Journal of Regional Studies*, vol. 1, no. 2, 2008, p. 47.
4. Ibid.
5. Ibid.

6. Ibid.
7. Ibid., p. 49.
8. Blum, John M. *The National Experience: A History of the United States.* 8th ed., San Diego, New York, Chicago, Atlanta, Washington D.C., London, Sydney, and Toronto, Cengage Learning, January 2, 1993. p. 824.
9. Rice, Connie Park. "'Don't Flinch nor Yield an Inch': J. R. Clifford and the Struggle for Equal Rights in West Virginia." *West Virginia History: A Journal of Regional Studies*, vol. 1, no. 2, 2008, pp. 45-46.
10. Ibid. p. 46.
11. Finkelman, Paul, and J. Clay Smith. "Not Only the Judges' Robes Were Black: African-American Lawyers as Social Engineers." *Stanford Law Review*, vol. 47, no. 1, 1994, p. 196. JSTOR, www.jstor.org/stable/1229224.
12. Ibid., p. 165.
13. "West Virginia's Early African American Lawyers" Excerpt from *Emancipation: The Making of the Black Lawyer 1844-1944* by J. Clay Smith, Jr. 1933, *Pioneer Press – The Souvenir Edition.* 2004-2006, www.jrclifford.org/images/JR%20Clifford%20and%20the%20Carrie%20Williams%20Case.pdf. p. 6.
14. Finkelman, Paul, and J. Clay Smith. "Not Only the Judges' Robes Were Black: African-American Lawyers as Social Engineers." *Stanford Law Review*, vol. 47, no. 1, 1994, p. 200. JSTOR, www.jstor.org/stable/1229224.
15. Ibid., p. 201.

16. Rice, Connie Park. "'Don't Flinch nor Yield an Inch': J. R. Clifford and the Struggle for Equal Rights in West Virginia." *West Virginia History: A Journal of Regional Studies*, vol. 1, no. 2, 2008, p. 46.
17. Finkelman, Paul, and J. Clay Smith. "Not Only the Judges' Robes Were Black: African-American Lawyers as Social Engineers." (November 1994). *Stanford Law Review*, Vol. 47, No. 1, November 1994. p. 182.
18. Ibid., p. 178.
19. Ibid., p. 180.
20. Rice, Connie Park. "'For Men and Measures: The Life and Legacy of Civil Rights Pioneer J.R. Clifford." *Eberly College of Arts and Sciences at West Virginia University*, 2007. pp. 1-2.
21. "Certain Dimensions of the Life & Times of J.R. Clifford." Excerpt from an article by Paul Ingram Clifford, J.R. Clifford's grandson, 1988, *Pioneer Press – The Souvenir Edition*. 2004-2006, www.jrclifford.org/images/JR%20Clifford%20and%20the%20Carrie%20Williams%20Case.pdf. p. 3.
22. Ibid.

Minor conflicting dates regarding key events in J. R. Clifford's life exist in some sources. Dates used in this work are derived from Connie Park Rice's "'For Men and Measures: The Life and Legacy of Civil Rights Pioneer J.R. Clifford" as well as the *J.R. Clifford An African American National Biography* entry also by Rice.

23. Rice, Connie Park. "'For Men and Measures: The Life and Legacy of Civil Rights Pioneer J.R. Clifford." *Eberly College of Arts and Sciences at West Virginia University*, 2007. p. 20.
24. Ibid., p. 22.
25. Ibid., p. 23.
26. Ibid., p. 26.
27. Ibid., pp. 22-23.
28. Ibid., p. 23.
29. Rodd, Thomas W. *Stories from West Virginia's Civil Rights History: A New Home for Liberty: J.R. Clifford and the Carrie Williams Case.* Charleston, WV, Quarrier Press, 2015. p. 26.
30. Rice, Connie Park. "'For Men and Measures: The Life and Legacy of Civil Rights Pioneer J.R. Clifford." *Eberly College of Arts and Science at West Virginia University*, 2007. pp. 23-24.
31. "Civil War Heritage Park." *Welcome To Camp Nelson*, www.campnelson.org/home.htm.
32. "J.R. Clifford - a Young Soldier at Camp Nelson, Kentucky." *Pioneer Press – The Souvenir Edition*. 2004-2006, www.jrclifford.org/images/JR%20Clifford%20and%20the%20Carrie%20Williams%20Case.pdf. p. 22.
33. "Civil War Heritage Park." *Welcome To Camp Nelson*, www.campnelson.org/home.htm.
34. "J.R. Clifford - a Young Soldier at Camp Nelson, Kentucky." *Pioneer Press – The Souvenir Edition*. 2004-2006

www.jrclifford.org/images/JR%20Clifford%20and%20the%20Carrie%20Williams%20Case.pdf. p. 22.
35. Ibid.
36. Ibid.
37. Rice, Connie Park. "'For Men and Measures: The Life and Legacy of Civil Rights Pioneer J.R. Clifford." *Eberly College of Arts and Sciences at West Virginia University*, 2007. p. 24.
38. Rice, Connie Park. *J.R. Clifford An African American National Biography*. Edited by Henry Louis Gates and Evelyn Brooks Higginbotham, vol. 2, Harvard and Oxford Press, 2008. p. 328.
39. Ibid.
40. Ibid.
41. Ibid., pp. 328-329.
42. *The J.R. Clifford Project*, www.jrclifford.org/
43. Rice, Connie Park. "'Don't Flinch nor Yield an Inch': J. R. Clifford and he Struggle for Equal Rights in West Virginia." *West Virginia History: A Journal of Regional Studies*, vol. 1, no. 2, 2008, p. 45.
44. Ibid., p. 46.
45. Ibid.
46. "J. R. Clifford." *West Virginia Archives & History*, www.wvculture.org/history/archives/blacks/clifford.html.
47. Rice, Connie Park. *J.R. Clifford An African American National Biography*. Edited by Henry Louis Gates and Evelyn Brooks Higginbotham, vol. 2, Harvard and Oxford Press, 2008. p. 328.

48. Rice, Connie Park. "'Don't Flinch nor Yield an Inch': J. R. Clifford and the Struggle for Equal Rights in West Virginia." *West Virginia History: A Journal of Regional Studies*, vol. 1, no. 2, 2008, p. 50.
49. Rice, Connie Park. *J.R. Clifford An African American National Biography.* Edited by Henry Louis Gates and Evelyn Brooks Higginbotham, vol. 2, Harvard and Oxford Press, 2008. p. 329.
50. Rice, Connie Park. "'For Men and Measures: The Life and Legacy of Civil Rights Pioneer J.R. Clifford." *Eberly College of Arts and Science at West Virginia University*, 2007. p. 58.
51. "Flick vs. Clifford." The Pioneer Press Vol. 4 Martinsburg, W.Va. October, 1886 No. 10, *Pioneer Press – The Souvenir Edition.* 2004-2006, www.jrclifford.org/images/JR%20Clifford%20and%20the%20Carrie%20Williams%20Case.pdf. p. 7.
52. Ibid.
53. Rice, Connie Park. "'For Men and Measures: The Life and Legacy of Civil Rights Pioneer J.R. Clifford." *Eberly College of Arts and Sciences at West Virginia University*, 2007. p. 60.
54. "Flick vs. Clifford." The Pioneer Press Vol. 4 Martinsburg, W.Va. October, 1886 No. 10, *Pioneer Press – The Souvenir Edition.* 2004-2006, www.jrclifford.org/images/JR%20Clifford%20and%20the%20Carrie%20Williams%20Case.pdf. p. 7.
55. Rice, Connie Park. "'Don't Flinch nor Yield an Inch': J. R. Clifford and the Struggle for Equal Rights in West

Virginia." *West Virginia History: A Journal of Regional Studies*, vol. 1, no. 2, 2008, p. 53.
56. Ibid., p. 45.
57. Finkelman, Paul, and J. Clay Smith. "Not Only the Judges' Robes Were Black: African-American Lawyers as Social Engineers." *Stanford Law Review*, vol. 47, no. 1, 1994, p. 180. JSTOR, www.jstor.org/stable/1229224.
58. Rice, Connie Park. "'Don't Flinch nor Yield an Inch': J. R. Clifford and the Struggle for Equal Rights in West Virginia." *West Virginia History: A Journal of Regional Studies*, vol. 1, no. 2, 2008, p. 57.
59. Ibid.
60. Ibid.
61. Ibid., p. 57.
62. Ibid., p. 61.
63. Ibid., p. 49.
64. Ibid., p.54.
65. Ibid.
66. Ibid., p. 53.
67. Ibid., p. 51.
68. Ibid., p.54.
69. Ibid.
70. Ibid., p.58.
71. Smith, Douglas C. "A West Virginia Dilemma: Martin v. Board Education of Education 1896." *WV Division of Culture and History*, vol. 40, no. 2, 1979, p. 3.
72. Reid, John Phillip. *An American Judge: Marmaduke Dent of West Virginia*. New York University Press, 1968. pp. 21-22.

73. Rice, Connie Park. "'Don't Flinch nor Yield an Inch': J. R. Clifford and the Struggle for Equal Rights in West Virginia." *West Virginia History: A Journal of Regional Studies*, vol. 1, no. 2, 2008, p. 58.
74. Rice, Connie Park. "'For Men and Measures: The Life and Legacy of Civil Rights Pioneer J.R. Clifford." *Eberly College of Arts and Sciences at West Virginia University*, 2007. p. 181.
75. Ibid., p. 209.
76. Smith, Lawrence. "Starcher Keeping Memory of State's First Black Attorney Alive." *West Virginia Record*, 5 Oct. 2006, wvrecord.com/stories/510589339-newsinator-starcher-keeping-memory-of-state-s-first-black-attorney-alive.
77. "Excerpts from 1915 Writings, September 18, 1915." *Pioneer Press – The Souvenir Edition*. 2004-2006, www.jrclifford.org/images/JR%20Clifford%20and%20the%20Carrie%20Williams%20Case.pdf. p. 20.
78. Rice, Connie Park. *J.R. Clifford An African American National Biography*. Edited by Henry Louis Gates and Evelyn Brooks Higginbotham, vol. 2, Harvard and Oxford Press, 2008. p. 329.
79. *Pioneer Press – The Souvenir Edition*. 2004-2006, www.jrclifford.org/images/JR%20Clifford%20and%20the%20Carrie%20Williams%20Case.pdf. p. 8.
80. "J. R. Clifford-A Fighting Rascal" Excerpt from *W.E.B. Du Bois: Biography of a Race, 1868-1919*, by David Levering Lewis, 1993. *Pioneer Press – The Souvenir Edition*.

2004-2006,
www.jrclifford.org/images/JR%20Clifford%20and%20the%20Carrie%20Williams%20Case.pdf. p. 1.
81. Rice, Connie Park. "'For Men and Measures: The Life and Legacy of Civil Rights Pioneer J.R. Clifford." *Eberly College of Arts and Sciences at West Virginia University*, 2007. p. 17.

CHAPTER SEVEN
Carrie Goes to Court

When Carrie Williams received her teaching contract that shortened the school year for the African American children at the Coketon Colored School to five months while retaining an eight-month calendar for white students, she faced a stark dilemma. After all, the odds were formidable, making it a safe conjecture that the all white school board anticipated little, if any, objection to its plan that affected only the black children of the Fairfax District. Despite a successful vote to increase taxes for educational purposes, the Tucker County Board of Education pursued an austerity program that negatively impacted African American children. West Virginia was not alone in establishing cost saving practices at the expense of black children. Frequently, school boards throughout the South attempted to slash funding to both black and white public schools. However, expenditures were cut as far as possible in black schools long before the board turned to the white schools. Despite laws to prevent this, it is unlikely that Tucker County was the only area in West Virginia where this occurred.[1] Clearly, the all white school board controlled by D C & C Co. expected acquiescence to its economic and social agenda. That expectation rested upon the reality of Carrie's life situation. Like their neighbors in the six towns of the Fairfax District, the Williams family's livelihood and relative prosperity were deeply intertwined within the concentric circles of influence generated by Davis Coal & Coke.

In particular, Thomas, as the largest of the six communities, embodied the image of the booming, fast growing company town that a mere ten years earlier had been a relative wilderness. Now due to D C & C Co., the Geisbergers opened a hotel, Feely & Wilson established a second store and William McGan sold freshly baked bread and confections at his bakery. Thomas also boasted two newspapers: the *Thomas Record*, a weekly, 1900-05, that had its own plant in town; and in 1905, a second newspaper, the *Thomas Sentinel* owned by R. D. Bennedetto and edited by W.B. Allen. Added to these publications was the only Italian newspaper in the state, *La Sentinella del West Virginia*, edited by Vincenzo Procopio.[2]

Local historian Thomas Nutter proudly proclaimed that the life of Thomas largely depended upon the coal industry, gratefully adding that D C & C Co., "pays as high wages as any company in the state, and furnishes steadier employment than almost any other company in the country."[3] In fact, Nutter not only praised Davis and his brother Thomas, but also dedicated his 1906 *History of Thomas "To Hon. THOMAS B. DAVIS, M. C., In Recognition of His Invaluable Services to the Town.*[4] This grateful acknowledgement also extended to Davis' West Virginia Central & Pittsburg Railroad as both a source of transportation and employment for the local population. Prosperity in Thomas and the surrounding area was inextricably woven into the corporate structure, clearly amplifying the definition of a company town and resulting in a proverbially grateful community. This only serves to underscore Carrie Williams' bravery in her decision to challenge a D C & C Co. controlled school board.

Coketon, located just steps away to the south of Thomas at the confluence of Synder Run and the North Fork of the Blackwater River, was the heart of industrial activity. At the center of this approximately one square mile thriving industrial town with a population of approximately 2500 were the Davis Coal & Coke corporate headquarters and the Buxton and Landstreet Company Store. The street moving downward half a mile from the main office and the company store to the banks of the Blackwater River led to the company housing for African American families as well as the Coketon Colored School built near the railroad tracks. This was also the site of nine coal mines and nearly one thousand coke ovens that operated two hundred and fifty days a year.

To the families who lived here and the children who attended the Coketon Colored School, the constant reverberation of the tipple, rattling as it funneled coal into the waiting railroad cars, was as familiar as Carrie Williams ringing her school bell. Smoke from locomotive engines and the pervasive gas from the coke ovens blended in with the ever present coal dust that permeated all in its wake. In 1892, 26 black students between 6 and 16 years of age attended the Coketon Colored School. This segment of the population grew, and according to the 1910 census, twenty African American families lived in Coketon or approximately two hundred and sixty-four African American people.[5] This was Carrie Williams' home community whose children's rights to fair educational opportunities were at the core of her fight in *Williams vs. the Tucker County Board of Education.*

In her quiet, steady advocacy for justice for the African American children in the Fairfax District, Carrie Williams became a formidable adversary, one who championed equal opportunity for all citizens in an era when Jim Crow reigned supreme. As W. E. B. Du Bois, Clifford's friend and cofounder of the Niagara Movement, assessed, "Of all the civil rights for which the world has struggled and fought for 5,000 years, the right to learn is undoubtedly the most fundamental. The freedom to learn has been bought by bitter sacrifice. And whatever we may think of the curtailment of other civil rights, we should fight to the last ditch to keep open the right to learn."[6] For Carrie Williams, this was a right that she and her family were prepared to defend regardless of any adverse repercussions that they might experience. Consequently, when presented with her teaching contract for the academic school year 1892-93, Carrie refused to sign despite repeated attempts by the school board to obtain her signature. However, the school board allowed Carrie Williams to teach at the Coketon Colored School without a signed contract.

As Carrie Williams later testified in court, "I knew the white school term was eight months, and *I saw counsel* and went on."[7] While this may seem a logical step, for African Americans in the Jim Crow era, this was no easy feat. At the time of Carrie Williams' case, only fourteen African American lawyers were admitted to the bar in West Virginia. Fortunately for her and the black children in the Fairfax District, John Robert Clifford was eager to argue this case against the segregated school system. Without his zealous outlook, it is unlikely that a black teacher would have been able to bring such a suit.[8] Believing that pervasive inequities existed in segregated schools that marked African Americans with a 'badge of inferiority,'[9] Clifford seized this opportunity to challenge these injustices in court. In his view, segregation was a direct violation of the 14th Amendment's due process and equal protection of the law clauses. Not only did Clifford now have a case that tested the deepening racial stratification that was occurring throughout the South and former border states, but also in Carrie Williams he had a brave plaintiff willing to pursue it.[10]

Although it is not clear how Carrie Williams found Clifford, it is likely that she and her husband Abraham, as educated African Americans, subscribed to the *Pioneer Press* in which Clifford advertised his legal services. Similarly, C. O. Strieby, the lawyer representing the Tucker County Board of Education of Fairfax District, promoted his services in the local Thomas paper, stating that his office was in the Bank Building in Davis.[11] Another likely connection is that Carrie Williams at some point met J. R. Clifford when she taught the children of Clifford's half brother James Hensom Clifford. Years later, Carrie and Abraham's daughter Nevada Williams Thompson, who died in the flu pandemic of 1918, was buried in an unmarked grave in the Rose Hill Cemetery in Thomas, not far from the gravesite of James Hensom Clifford.[12]

As Carrie Williams engaged J. R. Clifford to represent her in this suit against the Tucker County Board of Education of Fairfax District, she initiated a campaign against the discrimination and injustice that she encountered. Now with Clifford as her attorney, Carrie steadfastly moved forward. Clifford's counsel was concise, advising his client to teach the same number of months as the white schools, a full eight months.[13] What becomes evident in Carrie Williams' later trial testimony is her perceptive understanding of West Virginia law regarding the education of African American children. That, coupled with her unfaltering determination to provide fair educational opportunities for her students despite the racially charged judicial climate of the Jim Crow era, is a testament to her belief in the American system of justice despite its flaws.

Although Carrie Williams had refused to sign her contract that specified a five-month term for the Coketon Colored School, she received her salary of $40 per month. However, payments from the school board ceased after five months. At that point, Harold Meyer, the Secretary of the Tucker County Board of Education and Vice-President of the Davis Coal & Coke Company, asked Carrie for her class register. When she refused to submit her class register and stated that she planned to continue teaching for the next three months, Meyer then advised her that she would not be paid for the extra three months and the school board would withhold $1.00 from her final payment for failure to turn in the class register. Over the next three months, Carrie did not receive any salary from the school board, and as J.R. Clifford had suggested, the family lived on their savings.

Now the stage was set for legal action. After completing the eight-month school term, Carrie Williams sought payment for the final three months plus the $1.00 fee only to be rejected by the board. On June 30, 1893, J. R. Clifford, along with A. G. Dayton, a prominent white Republican attorney, filed a lawsuit against the Tucker County Board of Education of Fairfax District on her behalf. At this time, black lawyers usually designated white attorneys as their associates. However, Dayton did not actually participate in the case. In a letter to the court, Clifford maintained that he "was the only attorney in the case" and in a postscript added, "Dayton's name appears in the record only through an act of courtesy."[14]

> S. B. ELKINS, President.
> T. B. DAVIS, Vice Pres.
>
> **Davis Coal and Coke Co.**
> Office of Genl. Manager
>
> F. J. Landstreet, General Manager.
>
> GENERAL OFFICE
> NO. BROADWAY NEW YORK
> AGENCIES:
> PIEDMONT, W.VA. | BALTIMORE, MD.
> WILMINGTON, DEL. | PHILADELPHIA, PA.
> TRENTON, N.J. | BOSTON, MASS.
>
> Thomas, W.Va., Aug 2 1893
>
> J. R. Clifford Esq.
> Martinsburg W.Va.
>
> Dear Sir
>
> I have your letter of July 31" making inquiries in regard to Mrs. Williams' claim for $120.00. The school fund of this district was divided according to section 18 of the school law and the colored people were allotted their share, which proportion gave them about $200.00. Mrs. Williams was engaged to teach this term and received her pay for the same at the close of the 5 months. She was notified to stop by the Trustee & B of E but persisted in teaching some time longer. How long I do not know as no reports were sent to this office. She was teaching without a contract & without authority from anybody and if she thinks she can make her claim by law, we shall be pleased to meet her at her earliest convenience

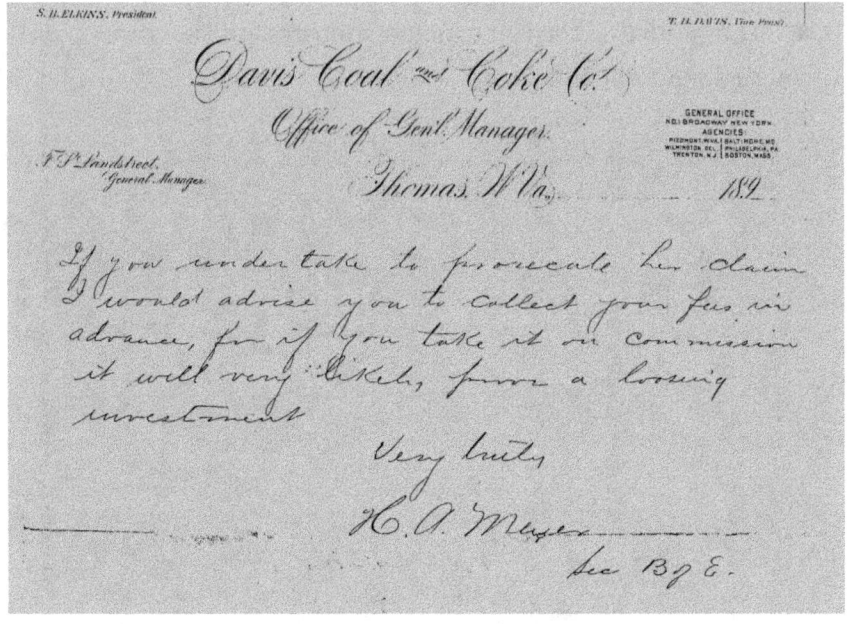

H.J. Meyer letter to J.R. Clifford, August 2, 1893
West Virginia University School of Law Archives

A few weeks later on August 2, 1893, Clifford received a letter from H. J. Meyer. In this correspondence written on Davis Coal & Coke Co. stationary, Meyer warned Clifford against taking legal action on behalf of Carrie Williams. "If you undertake to prosecute her claim I would advise you to collect your fees in advance, for if you take it on commission it will very likely prove a losing investment."[15] Clearly, Meyer was suggesting that the real future economic losses that Clifford might experience would be as a result of D C & C Co.'s anger over what it regarded as interference in its mining empire. Unfortunately for Meyer, this advice fell on deaf ears. Clifford's earlier newspaper and legal battles had inured him to intimidation. As the school board refused to pay his client's fees, consequently, "In November of 1893, Clifford filed a lawsuit on behalf of Williams claiming the Fairfax District School Board owed Carrie Williams one hundred twenty dollars for teaching the colored school at Thomas for three months plus one dollar withheld from her monthly wages for not making out a report," (failure to submit her class register).[16] However, the case took two years to arrive before a judge.

In 1895, the trial in the case of *Carrie Williams vs. the Board of Education of the Fairfax District* was held before the Circuit Court of Tucker County, the Honorable Joseph T. Hoke presiding. Most importantly, this was a jury trial, a jury of Carrie's peers. Although women did not yet sit on juries, throughout his career, Clifford had emphatically advocated for African American men as jurors, a civil right guaranteed by the 1879 *Strauder vs. West Virginia* case. Furthermore, during the 1890s, the already vital, growing Mountaineer community of Tucker County experienced a dramatic population growth. Included among the citizens from other states was a significant increase in the number of African Americans now residing in the six towns of the Fairfax District. In addition, Carrie's jury would have been chosen from new citizens – Italians, Lithuanians, Hungarians, and Poles, - who were among the many recent newcomers to the United States. All of these residents lived and worked together in the mining towns of Tucker County. A jury selected from this diverse pool of Carrie Williams' fellow citizens was about to decide what constitutes a "fair and legal" education for the black children in the Coketon Colored School.

Presiding over this trial was Justice Joseph T. Hoke. Earlier in his career as a state senator, not only did he cast the deciding vote for the charter that established Storer College, a normal school for African Americans, but also he continued as a long-term trustee of the institution. Indeed, J. R. Clifford was among the early graduates of Storer. Knowing Hoke's political leanings, it is probable that Clifford's advice to Carrie Williams to teach the full eight-month term was premised on his expectation that this trial would be before a judge sympathetic to the need for African American education.[17] As a senator, Hoke had also played a critical role in West Virginia's timely ratification of the 15th Amendment. Now as Circuit Court Justice, Hoke presided over the *Williams vs. the Board of Education of Fairfax District* case.

Legally, Carrie Williams was suing the Tucker County Board of Education for her salary for the three additional months that she taught at the Coketon Colored School. However, for Carrie Williams, this case was truly about fairness and justice under the rule of law. Likewise, J. R. Clifford, while representing his client for back pay, was really arguing the legality of the Board's decision under West Virginia law, and in a larger framework, the due process and equal protection of the law clauses of the 14th Amendment. Opposing counsel, C. O. Strieby, who had once been a teacher at the Thomas grade school for white children, represented the Board's contractual argument. In his view, the Board had paid Carrie Williams her salary for the five-month period despite her failure to sign a contract. Consequently, she was not entitled to extended pay since the Board had determined that the colored school term was only five months.

In addition to the positions of the opposing attorneys, the *Williams* case has a specific historical context within West Virginia law regarding public education. While the revised 1872 state constitution of West Virginia mandated segregated schools, state law required "the trustees of every sub-district to establish therein one or more primary schools for colored persons between the ages of six and twenty-one" and that "such schools so established shall be subject to the same regulations as are provided for the schools for the white children."[18] Initially, a school must be established if there were more than thirty black students in the district. However, that number was soon reduced to fifteen students.[19] Gradually, the required number of African American children was lowered to ten, allowing districts to establish more schools for black children. Carrie Williams' suit demanding a "fair – and legal" school term for her students rested clearly within the framework of state established mandates for public education.

As the bailiff called the court to session that day in Parsons, West Virginia, county seat and location of the Tucker County Courthouse, the trial officially began. Prior to the admission of the jury, Judge Hoke had identified himself as a long-term trustee of Storer College, asking the attorneys if either felt that he should recuse himself because Clifford was a graduate of the college. Since neither attorney objected to Judge Hoke's role as a trustee, the jury was summoned and seated. The list of witnesses to testify was short: Carrie Williams and Harold Meyer, Secretary of the Tucker County Board of Education.

(Quotations from the jury trial are taken from Thomas Rodd's adaptation of the original trial transcript as presented in Rodd, Thomas. *Stories from West Virginia's Civil Rights History: A New Home for Liberty: J.R. Clifford and the Carrie Williams Case.* Charleston, WV, Quarrier Press, 2015.)[20]

As J. R. Clifford called the plaintiff Carrie Williams to the stand, testimony began. Answering Clifford's questions, Carrie stated her occupation as the teacher at the Coketon Colored School and testified that she did not have a written contract with the Tucker County Board of Education for the academic year 1892-93. "The School Board refused to give me a contract for eight months like the contracts they gave the white schoolteachers. The Board wanted me to sign a contract for only five months. But I would not sign it."[21] When asked what happened at the conclusion of five months, Carrie testified that she kept on teaching without pay. "My husband and I used our savings to live, so I could give my pupils a fair and legal education... I am still owed three months' salary – one hundred and twenty dollars." When Clifford asked Carrie, "So it was solely a desire for a fair education for your students that motivated you?" Carrie's response was decisive. "Fair - and legal."[22] Clearly, Carrie understood that the laws in West Virginia demanded an equal educational calendar for her students. While her primary motivation was equity for African American children, this naturally extended to the concept of salary parity for white and black teachers. Shortening the black school year also meant a reduced salary for African American teachers.

As Clifford concluded his questioning, C. O. Strieby approached the witness stand and began his questioning of Carrie. After acknowledging that Mr. Meyer, the School Board Secretary, had informed her that she would not receive further payments after the conclusion of the five-month school term, Carrie further confirmed that she had not complied with his demand to give him the class register. At this point, Carrie produced the completed class register, and rather than giving it immediately to Strieby, she began reading its substance. "We covered eight subjects: orthography, reading, penmanship, arithmetic, grammar, history, geography, and language lessons." When Strieby questioned that her motivation for teaching the

Teacher's Monthly Summary signed by Carrie Williams, May 26, 1893
West Virginia University School of Law Archives

three additional months was that the white schools had an eight-month calendar, not because she had a contract for that length of time, Carrie responded affirmatively, adding, "And I believe it is the law."[23] For Strieby and the Tucker County Board of Education, this case was anchored solely in contractual law. Clifford then moved to have the class register admitted into evidence so that the jury could examine what Carrie had accomplished in the eight-month school term. Overruling Strieby's objection that the class register was irrelevant to the issue at hand, Hoke admitted it as evidence that the jury could consider in their deliberations.

The next witness was Harold Meyer who, in response to the question asking him to state his name and occupation, identified himself initially as vice-president of Davis Coal & Coke Co. and then as Secretary of the School Board. After Clifford established that the School Board set the property taxes for the district and that those taxes paid for all of the schools within the district, white and colored, he went on to question Meyer as to why in the 1892-93 school year did the white schools receive funds for eight months while the colored school was only allocated funds for five months. Meyer's response was that, "it was simple arithmetic. We calculated the number of white children in the district and the number of colored children. There were less colored children, so their share of the taxes only allowed for five months of school."[24] To Meyer, this was a straightforward, logical explanation.

Knowing that the citizens of the Fairfax District had voted for a tax increase for education, but only the "colored" school year had been shortened as an austerity factor in the school budget, Clifford then posed the question, "Could you not raise the property taxes, so as to pay for a full eight-month term of school for both white and colored children?" Meyer's response again seemed like basic logic to him. "Why... why, to do that would cost more for each colored pupil than for each white pupil, because there are less colored." According to Meyer, "that would be entirely irregular."[25] Clifford then pursued his line of questioning, asking whether or not the Davis Coal & Coke Co. "owns large tracts of property in Tucker County," and most importantly, "pays most of the school property tax?"[26] Despite Strieby's objection to the relevance of this question, Judge Hoke allowed it, agreeing with Clifford's response that the question demonstrated the witness' motive. Meyer then reluctantly responded that Davis Coal and Coke Company did pay a large portion of the property tax, allowing Clifford to demonstrate a corporate financial motive for the shortened black school term to the jury.

On cross-examination, Strieby asked Meyer if his service as the Secretary of the Board of Education was solely an act of public service. Meyer quickly affirmed that it was, and then added, "And on behalf of Davis Coal and Coke Company, I can tell you that our company has a strong interest in maintaining an educated and contented work force."[27] After Strieby then asked Meyer if he believed that he was acting within the law as he understood it, Meyer replied affirmatively only to have Clifford object to the relevancy of what Meyer thought the law was. Hoke agreed with Clifford. Stating that sufficient evidence had been presented to demonstrate that Carrie Williams should be paid $120.00 for her "teaching services," Clifford rested his case. Likewise, Strieby rested, stating that since Mrs. Williams had no contract, she was not owed any sum of money.[28]

Judge Hoke commenced the next stage of the trial by instructing the jury. "The court instructs you that the Constitution of the State of West Virginia provides that whites and colored shall not be educated in the same school. The law also requires the Board of Education to establish schools for the equivalent education of the colored children in the District. The court instructs you that a person may not seek payment without a contract. But it is also true that every contract must comply with the law."[29] Hoke further advised the jurors that their verdict must be based on the fundamental legal principles that he had presented.

Hoke then allowed both lawyers to make their closing arguments to the jury. Clifford's final remarks went to the essence of the case. In his mind, the issue was simple: jurors must decide whether or not the School Board must follow the law of the state of West Virginia that required the Board to "provide the necessary funds for the colored children's schooling - even if it means that the Davis Coal & Coke Company will pay more in taxes."[30] Clifford went on to affirm that Carrie Williams had abided by the law, earning her salary each day of the three months in question while "it is the School Board that deviated from the law."[31] In his eloquent closing, Clifford articulated a key principle of American law. "No matter what the color of a person's skin is, here in America, all workers deserve full and fair pay for the work that they do."[32] While Clifford was speaking to a jury in 1895, those words rooted in the original intention of the 14th Amendment were to be echoed in equal pay for equal work court cases across the United States in the latter part of the twentieth century.

As Strieby addressed the jury, he stressed that this was a case about contract. "Of course, I ask you to follow the law. But the law does not contradict our common sense."[33] He went on to state that only work performed with a contract demands payment. "My client, the Board of Education, set the term for the colored school at five months – and no one challenged the Board's action! So, Mrs. Williams cannot make her claim in this court."[34] Of course, what the jurors knew, just as Carrie Williams knew, no one challenged a Board of Education controlled by Davis Coal & Coke Company, especially if they wanted to continue in its employment complete with company housing.

The jury found in favor of the plaintiff in the amount of $120.00. After hearing of C.O. Strieby's decision to appeal the case, Judge Hoke then entered a judgment for the plaintiff in the amount of $120.00 with interest at ten percent per annum. Although Carrie Williams and J. R. Clifford knew that an appeal was before them, for the time being, they had won, even if temporarily, a decisive battle in the fight for equal educational opportunities for African American children and equal pay for their teachers.

As J. R. Clifford submitted his brief in the *Williams vs. the Tucker County Board of Education of Fairfax District* case to the West Virginia Supreme Court of Appeals, he was acutely aware of the political and social climate of the time. His recent September of 1896 appearance before this same appellate court in *Martin vs. the Morgan County Board of Education* had been unsuccessful on the surface. In that case, the plaintiff, Thomas Martin, sought admission for his five children to the only school available to his family, a school for white children. Clifford, seeking to test the constitutionality of the segregated school law in West Virginia, had argued that such a system violated the original intent of the due process and equal protection of the law clauses of the 14th Amendment only to have his premise rejected by the West Virginia high court.

In his appellate argument, Clifford acknowledged that Article XII, Section 8, of the West Virginia Constitution of 1872 established segregated schools for white and black students. However, he argued that when a school board failed to provide equal facilities for white and African American children such a law establishing segregated schools "is contrary to the 14th Amendment and is void." Clifford further maintained that the Martin children should therefore be admitted to the white school.[35] However, in the Martin opinion written by Judge Marmaduke Dent, the State Supreme Court of Appeals asserted that the West Virginia State Constitution held dominance over the 14th Amendment of the United States Constitution. In light of the recent May of 1896 *Plessy vs. Ferguson* United States Supreme Court decision, Clifford had little realistic recourse of appeal. Similar to the lower court's verdict, the legal system left the Martin children with no access to public education. However, due to the negative publicity and the cost of litigation, the Morgan County Board of Education created a school for African American children. While Clifford was unsuccessful in enabling black children to attend a white school in the Martin case, he brought attention to the need for black schools in areas where few black students lived.

Despite the court's opinion, the Martin case constitutes the first legal attack on segregated public schools in West Virginia and certainly one of the first legal challenges to segregated schools in the South. Regardless of Judge Dent's declaration that the State Constitution of West Virginia superseded the 14th Amendment of the United States Constitution, Clifford's argument in the Martin case established a significant legal precedent by invoking the 14th Amendment's admonition that all citizens are entitled to the equal protection of the law, a precedent that twentieth century lawyers later successfully used in the civil rights movement.[36] Now on June 11, 1898, J. R. Clifford found himself and his client, Carrie Williams, in the same court, arguing before Judge Dent who, in conjunction with other appellate justices, would assess the validity of Clifford's legal arguments in the *Williams* case.

Just as the early history of West Virginia uniquely mirrors national debates, the background of Judge Marmaduke Dent also reflects these multifaceted themes. Born in Monongalia County, Virginia on April 18, 1849, Dent was still a boy as the tumultuous events of the Civil War unfolded. His mother, Mary Caroline Roberts was a native of New York and his maternal grandfather, Dr. D. W. Roberts, was an abolitionist and a delegate to the Republican Convention in Chicago that nominated Abraham Lincoln for President in 1860. His father, Marshall Dent, was the proprietor and editor of the Morgantown *Virginia Weekly Star* from 1856 to 1862, a newspaper that favored compromise in order to save the Union. However, as tensions heightened, Dent became a strong Unionist, changing the motto of his newspaper to "The Federal Union - it must and shall be preserved" and supported the Northern Democratic candidate, Stephen Douglas, in the 1860 presidential election.

Subsequently, as a representative of Monongalia County at the 1861 Virginia Secession Convention, Dent, together with Waitman T. Willey, voted against secession. In his newspaper editorials, he railed against eastern Virginians' betrayal of the western part of the state by "attempting to hitch her to a Cotton Confederacy" and predicted the inevitable separation from "their Eastern brethren."[37] Dent then attended the First Wheeling

Convention that authorized a new convention pending approval of Virginia's secession by the May 23, 1861, referendum. Marshall Dent remained a staunch Unionist who later became the circuit court clerk in Monongalia County and was admitted to the West Virginia bar in 1881.

Judge Marmaduke Dent
Image Source: Bench and Bar of West Virginia

Although Marshall Dent enjoyed a career as an editor, court clerk and lawyer, he was not a financial success. Consequently, in 1867, when Marmaduke Dent enrolled in the newly formed West Virginia University located in his hometown of Morgantown, he needed financial assistance from his uncle, Francis Chalfant, a member of the Board of Regents.[38] After receiving the first B.A. (1870) and M.A. (1873) degrees awarded by the university, Dent served as the inaugural president of its alumni association, still named for him. After graduation, Dent taught in West Virginia public schools until 1873 when he became a deputy clerk of the circuit and county court. During this time, Dent studied law, and in 1875, was admitted to the Taylor County Bar at Grafton where he practiced for nearly twenty years as well as holding several offices before his election to the West Virginia Supreme Court of Appeals in 1892. Serving until 1904, Dent, a staunch Democrat, lost his bid for reelection in a Republican electoral wave as a result of the popularity of incumbent presidential candidate, Theodore Roosevelt. After retiring to his home in Grafton, two years later, Dent ran for the United States Congress only to lose this bid in the 1906 Republican groundswell that won all five West Virginia Congressional seats.[39] Three years later, Marmaduke Dent died at his home in Grafton on September 11, 1909.

Described as possessing a judicial temperament with an intelligent and carefully trained mind, Dent was also known for his diligence and capacity for hard work. As West Virginia rapidly embraced the industrial era, Dent often voiced the minority opinion of the court, particularly in an era in which corporations held extensive influence. Dent firmly believed that "the law had created corporations so why deny it (the law) power to define and enforce steps necessary to curtail whatever hazards they may pose for the general public."[40] Clearly identifying with the populist leanings of his time, he was more likely to hold the railroads to a higher standard than the pro-industry majority on the court. In his 1897 opinion in *Scott vs. Chesapeake & Ohio Railway Company*, Dent describes the solicitous role that the court may play in protecting the more vulnerable in society. "One of the foundation stones of civil government is the protection of the weak against oppressive, willful conduct of the strong, and this is a principle that should be most rigidly enforced against powerful corporations who derive their existence and strength wholly from the government."[41]

Similarly, in *Raines vs. Chesapeake & Ohio Railway Company*, Dent sided with a "trespasser" on the railroad tracks killed by an oncoming train. Here, in contrast to the majority of the Court, Dent argued that corporations who enjoy special privilege have a duty to take special precautions; "what constitutes trespass on purely private property should not automatically be trespass on property belonging to certain public franchises."[42] Dent biographer, John Reid, asserts that "from the perspective of the twentieth century this doctrine of special care looms as Dent's most important contribution to West Virginia jurisprudence."[43] For Dent, protecting individual rights translated into curbing what he regarded as overreaching corporate power. Such beliefs may have made him more sympathetic to the injustice that the black students would have suffered as a result of the Davis Coal and Coke Company's influence on the Board of Education's decision to shorten the Coketon Colored School term.

Clifford, now in his second appearance before the West Virginia Supreme Court of Appeals, argued that the 1895 Tucker County Circuit Court decision should stand. Addressing the contractual issue first, Clifford claimed that "by law, that boards of education could waive written contracts with teachers. If the boards chose to do so, and still received the benefit of their teaching, they were required to pay for teacher services even without a written contract."[44] Secondly, Clifford presented the broader legal concern of this case: the law of the State of West Virginia "justified Carrie Williams's decision not to sign a contract if it violated the purpose and intent of the West Virginia Constitution calling for 'separate but equal' schools."[45] Alternatively, Strieby's argument rested upon a contractual triad: first of all, Carrie Williams had no written contract; secondly, state law does not allow for an implied contract; and thirdly, Carrie was not owed payment since she had voluntarily taught for three months.[46] After hearing arguments from both sides, the judges began their deliberations.

Five months later on November 16, 1898, the West Virginia Supreme Court of Appeals delivered its ruling, upholding the Tucker County Circuit Court's 1895 decision in *Williams vs. the Tucker County Board of Education of Fairfax District*. In the majority opinion, Judge Marmaduke Dent clearly delineated the Court's views. The high court dismissed the board's argument that Carrie Williams had worked without a signed contract, stating: "After the service has been rendered in a satisfactory manner... and the board has recognized and approved it by receiving her monthly reports, and paying her five months of salary, it is too late for them to object that her appointment was not in writing."[47]

Most importantly, Dent then addressed the Board of Education's attempt to impose a five-month term for African American students while funding eight months of education for white students. First, Dent stated that the law of West Virginia does not authorize boards of education to discriminate between white and colored schools in the same district as to the length of the term to be taught. Secondly, Judge Dent then explicated the school population issue in this case; "the trustees (of the school board) had not established a primary school as required by Section 17, chapter 45, Code, the enumeration of colored children being twenty-six." As Justice Dent stated, under West Virginia law, the number of black students, twenty-six in the Fairfax District, mandated a primary school. However, despite the fact that "the people of the district having voted for an eight months' school, the board arbitrarily determined the white schools should run eight months, and the colored school only five months."[48] In doing this, the school board had granted the black children their pro rata share (proportional share) of the funding under section 18 of the statute. The Court found that the school board's attempt to assign the "Colored children their pro rata share of funding... is directly in the face of the positive mandatory requirement of the statute, and it is contrary to public policy... (section 17, chapter 45, Code)."[49] Here, the Court clearly found that Secretary of the Board Meyer's explanation of the allocation of funds for the Coketon Colored School to be an illegal action in direct violation of West Virginia law. Ironically, Meyer had confidently outlined this pro rata allocation of funds in his pretrial letter to Clifford, a letter that had also insinuated the possible negative financial consequences of representing Carrie Williams.

Justice Dent then addressed the underlying racial issues in the Tucker County Board's decision to shorten the school term for African American children. "This distinction on the part of the board, being clearly illegal, and a discrimination made merely on account of color, should be treated as a nullity, as being contrary to public policy and good morals." Furthermore, Dent elaborated the Court's belief that, "If any discrimination as to education should be made, it should be favorable to, and not against, the colored people. Held in the bondage of slavery, and continued in a low moral and intellectual condition, for a long period of years, and then clothed at once, without preparation, with full citizenship, in this great republic... the future welfare, prosperity and peace of our people demand that this benighted race should be elevated by education."[50] While Dent's paternalistic language suggests "the white man's burden" and may have been offensive to Clifford,[51] the intent of the sentiments may have resonated with the beliefs of Judge Joseph Hoke who had personally witnessed the refugee situation occurring in the eastern panhandle of West Virginia at the conclusion of the Civil War as thousands of freedmen and their families sought food, shelter and education.

In the fast growing racial stratification sanctioned by law in states below the Mason - Dixon Line in the 1890s, Judge Dent's opinion is fortunately "out of place" for African American children and their teachers in West Virginia. His admonition may have, to some extent, foreshadowed "the modern practice of affirmative action."[52] In upholding the Tucker County's Circuit Court decision, Justice Dent concluded with an eloquent reminder that the Great American Experiment rests upon the rule of law. "A nation that depends on its wealth is a depraved nation, while moral purity and intellectual progress alone can preserve the integrity of free institutions, and the love of true liberty, under the protection of equal laws, in the hearts of the people."[53]

Dent's eloquent opinion in the Williams case appears dramatically at variance with his denial of a writ of mandamus in the Martin case where he rejected Clifford's equal protection and due process argument by stating that the West Virginia constitution held dominance over the 14th Amendment of the United States Constitution. However, as biographer John Reid explains, "Dent's place was post-Reconstruction West Virginia and his time was long before the fourteenth amendment had become the cornerstone of civil rights." Consequently, Judge Dent did not discuss civil rights, in part because he and his colleagues had only "shaded gleanings that the subject existed."[54] Dent's explanation of the misconstrued allowance of pro rata sharing rather than the funding of a primary school for a community that clearly had twenty-six black students allows the Court to mandate an equal school year for the African American children in Coketon without addressing the constitutionality of segregated schools. In contrast, Clifford's arguments rooted in the 14th Amendment reflect not only an understanding of the original intent of the Radical Republicans who crafted it, but also foreshadow the modern civil rights movement of all Americans, black and white alike.

The victory in *Williams vs. the Tucker County Board of Education* had far-reaching implications. As the first case in the United States to determine that discrimination based upon race alone is illegal, the *Williams* ruling is an extraordinary triumph in an era marred by the implementation of Jim Crow laws across the South and beyond. In particular, as historian Ancella Bickley emphasizes, West Virginia blacks felt empowered to seek redress in a court of law, making this "an interesting commentary" on the role of this state in the African American civil rights movement.[55] Not only did the *Williams* decision guarantee an equal school session for African American children in Coketon, but it also set a standard for school term equality throughout the state. In addition, the *Williams* case provided pay parity for their teachers, establishing this pivotal decision as a benchmark in the history of civil rights and equality in West Virginia.

The *Williams* verdict remained a rare achievement despite the discrepancies that continued to exist within educational opportunities in the state. Although West Virginia law did not provide equality for black students in the quality and quantity of facilities, materials, and administrative supervision that white students experienced,[56] victory in the Williams case, particularly for the black children attending a full eight-month school session throughout West Virginia, afforded a much fairer educational opportunity than what was envisioned by the Board of Education of the Fairfax District. At the same time, this court case impacted migration to the state as African Americans seeking better educational opportunities for their children now called the Mountain State their home. Furthermore, since the *Williams* decision guaranteed an equal school term for teachers as well as students, well-qualified black teachers sought employment in West Virginia, augmenting an already vital African American middle class within the state as well as indirectly influencing pay scales in neighboring states.

In addition to its legal ramifications, this landmark case is a testament not only to Carrie's bravery in confronting an ill conceived attempt to rob African American children of their educational rights, but also to the sense of fairness and justice that this Appalachian community exhibits. In siding with the plaintiff, Carrie Williams, the jurors of Tucker County made a resounding statement affirming the rights of their African American neighbors. In an age of escalating Jim Crow assaults, a brave teacher and a panel of ordinary citizens from atop the Allegheny Mountains demonstrate the promise of justice that American law strives to actualize. Most importantly, Carrie Williams' courageous decision to confront this injustice depicts the power of the individual to prevent a present inequity as well as its pernicious spread when unchallenged. However, until recently, the national importance of this landmark litigation has remained obscured, largely due to the earlier U. S. Supreme Court decision in *Plessy vs. Ferguson*. As West Virginia historian Connie Park Rice attests, "the *Williams* case provided southern blacks with a rare victory, and a small beacon of light in what historian Rayford W. Logan has described as the "nadir" of African-American history."[57]

For J. R. Clifford whose life had been spent in the pursuit of equal justice under the law, success in *Williams vs. the Tucker County Board of Education* provided an enhanced impetus in his continuing struggle for full civil rights for African Americans. As attorney and Clifford specialist Thomas Rodd affirms, "J. R. Clifford was a noble human being who transcended the archaic and misguided concept of race. He was unyielding in his struggle for justice for all. He is a role model for all who seek to build a better world."[58] Despite the escalating onslaught of discrimination and intolerance, Clifford's accomplishment in the *Williams* case bolstered him in his ongoing struggle against what must have seemed at times as overwhelming attempts to relegate African Americans to second-class citizenship. Furthermore, as a founding member of the Niagara Movement, Clifford helped to establish the basis of the twentieth century civil rights movement, a movement that effectively argued the far-reaching implications of the equal protection of the law clause of the 14th Amendment in the *Brown vs. the Board of Education of Topeka, Kansas* case. In this verdict, J. R. Clifford's earlier advocacy of the 14th Amendment's equal protection of the rights of all citizens, black and white, finally found vindication. Although Clifford would not live to relish this victory, it is a lasting tribute to his valiant crusade for black equal rights. Perhaps one of the most important results of the *Williams* decision is that it sustained J. R. Clifford in a time period that had so few successes for African Americans in their quest for full citizenship.

However, the victory in *Williams vs. the Tucker County Board of Education* ultimately belongs to Carrie Williams. Without her courage, strength and determination, the African American children of Coketon would have suffered a true injustice. What emerges in her story is the portrait of a strong woman, unafraid to challenge the most powerful economic and political entity in her world in order to ensure "fair - and legal" educational opportunities for her own children and her students, present and future. The *Williams* verdict that mandated that the Tucker County School Board provide equal school terms and equal pay regardless of color established the standard for African American education in West Virginia. Despite the legalization of second-class citizenship in the Jim Crow era, West Virginia stood alone amidst the southern and former border states, striking a distinctly positive note in the ongoing struggle for African American equality. In a racially stratified era sanctioned by the separate but equal doctrine of the *Plessy vs. Ferguson* decision, Carrie Williams, through her brave, spirited action, positively impacted the lives of thousands of African American children and their teachers throughout West Virginia. While segregated schools continued until the 1954 Supreme Court's ruling in the

Brown decision, Carrie's current and future students and their counterparts across the state attended the same school term as white students and their teachers experienced pay parity with white teachers throughout West Virginia.

Williams V. Board of Education Case
West Virginia Historical Marker
In front of Tucker County Courthouse, Parsons, West Virginia

In her action against the Tucker County Board of Education, Carrie Williams did not seek the spotlight or the acclaim of the townspeople. What she did seek was equal justice for all under the rule of law. Although little is known of Carrie after this landmark case, research indicates that the Williams family continued to live in Coketon until 1913 when Abraham died. Subsequently, Carrie and her younger children joined her older sons in Chicago where she lived until her death on January 22, 1930.[59] Hers is a life to be celebrated as a wife, a mother, a teacher, and an advocate for social justice. Carrie's achievement is a powerful example of what an individual may accomplish in choosing to fight injustice. This is not only her victory, but also a lasting testament to her belief in the rule of law and equal opportunity for all, black and white alike, in the pursuit of the promise of the Great American Experiment.

1. Rice, Connie Park. "'Don't Flinch nor Yield an Inch': J. R. Clifford and the Struggle for Equal Rights in West Virginia." *West Virginia History: A Journal of Regional Studies*, vol. 1, no. 2, 2008, p. 51.
2. Nutter, T. *Thomas, West Virginia: History, Progress and Development.* Parsons, W. Va., McClain Print. Co., 1906. pp. 15 – 16.
3. Ibid., p. 33.
4. Ibid. Dedication Page
5. Halderman, Lori. "Friends of Blackwater." Newsletter June 2012. *Visit Historic Coketon* p. 6.
6. Du Bois, William, *Pioneer Press Souvenir Edition*, 12 Aug. 2006, www.jrclifford.org/images/PioneerPressCentEdition.pdf. p. 16.

7. Rice, Connie Park. "'Don't Flinch nor Yield an Inch': J. R. Clifford and the Struggle for Equal Rights in West Virginia." *West Virginia History: A Journal of Regional Studies*, vol. 1, no. 2, 2008, p. 52.
8. Finkelman, Paul and J. Clay Smith. "Not Only the Judges' Robes Were Black: African-American Lawyers as Social Engineers" (November 1994). *Stanford Law Review*, Vol. 47, No. 1, November 1994. p. 193.
9. Rice, Connie Park. "'Don't Flinch nor Yield an Inch': J. R. Clifford and the Struggle for Equal Rights in West Virginia." *West Virginia History: A Journal of Regional Studies*, vol. 1, no. 2, 2008, p. 51.
10. Ibid., p. 52.
11. Nutter, T. *Thomas, West Virginia: History, Progress and Development.* Parsons, W.Va., McClain Print. Co., 1906. Business Directory.
12. "Friends of Blackwater." Newsletter *Blackwater Heroine Carrie Williams– Her Story Shared by Her Descendants*, October 2012 & *Historic Rose Hill Cemetery*, March 2017.
13. Rice, Connie Park. "'Don't Flinch nor Yield an Inch': J. R. Clifford and the Struggle for Equal Rights in West Virginia." *West Virginia History: A Journal of Regional Studies*, vol. 1, no. 2, 2008, p. 51.
14. Ibid., p. 54.
15. Ibid., p. 55.
16. Ibid.
17. Ibid., p. 52.

18. Podvia, Mark W. "Williams v. Board of Education of Fairfax District: Bringing a Long-Forgotten West Virginia Case to Life." *Unbound: A Review of Legal History and Rare Books Journal of the Legal History and Rare Books Series Interest Section of the American Association of Law Libraries*, vol. 8, 2015, pp. 31–32.
19. Engle, Stephen D. "Mountaineer Reconstruction: Blacks in the Political Reconstruction of West Virginia." *The Journal of Negro History*, vol. 78, no. 3, 1993, p. 146.
20. Rodd, Thomas. *Stories from West Virginia's Civil Rights History: a New Home for Liberty: J.R. Clifford and the Carrie Williams Case.* Charleston, WV, Quarrier Press, 2015.
21. Ibid., p. 52.
22. Ibid., p. 53.
23. Ibid., p. 54.
24. Ibid., p. 56.
25. Ibid.
26. Ibid.
27. Ibid., p. 57.
28. Ibid., p. 58.
29. Ibid., p. 59.
30. Ibid.
31. Ibid., p.60.
32. Ibid.
33. Ibid.
34. Ibid. p. 61.
35. Rice, Connie Park. "'Don't Flinch nor Yield an Inch': J. R. Clifford and the Struggle for Equal Rights in West

Virginia." *West Virginia History: A Journal of Regional Studies*, vol. 1, no. 2, 2008, pp. 58- 59.
36. Ibid.
37. Gunter, Donald W. *Education @ Library of Virginia*, www.lva.virginia.gov/public/dvb/.
38. Reid, John Phillip. *An American Judge: Marmaduke Dent of West Virginia*. New York University Press, 1968, p. 7.
39. Ibid., p. 15.
40. Ibid., p. 58.
41. "Judge Marmaduke Dent." *Pioneer Press Souvenir Edition*, 12 Aug. 2006, www.jrclifford.org/images/PioneerPressCentEdition.pdf. p. 23.
42. Reid, John Phillip. *An American Judge: Marmaduke Dent of West Virginia*. New York University Press, 1968, p. 58.
43. Ibid., p. 134.
44. Rice, Connie Park. "'Don't Flinch nor Yield an Inch': J. R. Clifford and the Struggle for Equal Rights in West Virginia." *West Virginia History: A Journal of Regional Studies*, vol. 1, no. 2, 2008, p. 60.
45. Ibid.
46. Ibid.
47. *The Southeastern Reporter*, vol. 31, West Publishing Company 1899, p. 985.
48. Ibid.
49. Ibid.
50. Ibid, p. 986.

51. Rice, Connie Park. "'Don't Flinch nor Yield an Inch': J. R. Clifford and the Struggle for Equal Rights in West Virginia." *West Virginia History: A Journal of Regional Studies*, vol. 1, no. 2, 2008, p. 62.
52. Lewis, Ronald L. "Marmduke Dent." *e-WV: The West Virginia Encyclopedia*. 27 December 2016. Web. 27 August 2017.
53. *The Southeastern Reporter*, vol. 31, West Publishing Company 1899, p. 985.
54. Reid, John Phillip. *An American Judge: Marmaduke Dent of West Virginia*. New York University Press, 1968, pp. 20-22.
55. *Transcript of Interview with Ancella Bickley, June 21, 1992, for the Film "West Virginia."* www.wvculture.org/history/wvmemory/filmtranscripts/wvbickley.html.
56. Rice, Connie Park. "'Don't Flinch nor Yield an Inch': J. R. Clifford and he Struggle for Equal Rights in West Virginia." *West Virginia History: A Journal of Regional Studies*, vol. 1, no. 2, 2008, p. 62.
57. Ibid., p.63.
58. Rodd, Thomas W. "J.R. Clifford, Esq. Heroic West Virginia Attorney and Civil Rights Pioneer." *The Advocate*, West Virginia Trial Lawyers Association, 2006, p. 19.
59. "Friends of Blackwater." Newsletter *Blackwater Heroine – Caroline Williams*, October 2014, p. 30.

Epilogue

Time and Place: Late November, 1898, in the Coketon Colored School, Coketon, West Virginia

Carrie walked quickly down the gravel path leading to the Coketon Colored School. There was a bounce in her step as she gazed at the rushing Blackwater River. A brisk wind scattered orange and red leaves alongside the railroad tracks, casting bright paint strokes amidst the ever present coal dust. She was greeted by the sound of the tipple long at work sending coal to the nearby railroad cars, a bustling scene as miners hard at work delved into waiting caverns, eager to fill their empty lorry cars.

As Carrie reached the door of the schoolhouse, she smiled at the pumpkins atop a makeshift display table - still thriving in the cool November air. "We will need a fire today," thought Carrie as she entered the large room of the school. Putting down her school bag, she placed her heavy wool cloak on the hook and thought about the letter she had just received. Remembering an earlier letter from the Tucker County School Board of six years ago, Carrie felt happy, confident in what she had accomplished.

Arriving home yesterday, Carrie had received J. R. Clifford's jubilant letter congratulating her on her victory in the West Virginia Supreme Court of Appeals. The court had sided with her, more importantly, she thought, with the black children of Coketon, ensuring a fair and legal school term for them. Remembering the past six years, Carrie felt a surge of relieved gratitude that her belief in the rule of law had been sustained, grateful that the children had this victory. "Maybe this is the real history lesson of the day," Carrie thought. She smiled, remembering her first meeting with J. R. Clifford, a robust man with seemingly endless energy, anxious, excited to fight for her and the black children in her schoolroom. Together they had forged ahead and now the children were the true victors. "And they will be here soon," thought Carrie. "Time to begin the school day."

Carrie Williams' struggle for "a fair and legal education" for her children and her students, present and future, was an integral part of her life, especially over the six years of litigation. Her quiet, steady advocacy for equal justice under the rule of law resulted in widespread consequences for the African American children of West Virginia where their rights to an equal school term were consistently respected despite increasingly hostile environments in the South and former border states. It is due to Carrie's brave decision to confront a gross inequity that not only prevented its occurrence, but also challenged its spread into other areas of life for African American citizens. In a time in American history marred by racial injustice, the *Williams* verdict remained a steady ray of hope as the nation grappled with the legacy of slavery.

Carrie Williams' life possesses the hallmarks of a genuine American heroic narrative. Not seeking acclaim, but rather quietly pursuing fairness for all under the rule of American law, she successfully challenged misguided ideas about race in the United States. At the same time, Carrie Williams continued her life as a wife, a mother, a teacher and a vital member of her integrated community in Appalachia. What is so remarkable about Carrie is that she saw the best in the American system despite so much evidence to the contrary in an era of legally sanctioned racial divisions of society. Her unfaltering belief in the rule of law sustained her in her advocacy for equal educational opportunities for African American children. The life of Carrie Williams is a testament to the power that an individual possesses to act upon fundamental beliefs and to successfully confront injustice against seemingly overwhelming odds. Once again, while this is Carrie's story set in West Virginia, it is a particularly American narrative that describes the unfolding Great Experiment as the United States strives to assure a fair and equitable society for all citizens. Carrie Williams is an American hero whose life is one to be celebrated and emulated.

This is Carrie's story, a true American heroic narrative.

Bibliography

"A Brief History of African Americans in West Virginia." *West Virginia Archives & History*, www.wvculture.org/history//africanamericans/ blacks.html.

"A Brief History of Coal and Health and Safety Enforcement in West Virginia." *West Virginia Office of Miners' Health Safety and Training, 2002.* www.wvminesafety.org/disaster.htm.

"African-American Population of Present-Day Counties in West Virginia in 1860." *West Virginia Archives & History*, www.wvculture.org/history///blackpop.html.

African Americans in Antebellum Ohio. Black, White and Beyond - An Interactive History, learn.uakron.edu/beyond/africanAm_antebellum.htm.

"A Timeline of African Americans in West Virginia." *West Virginia Archives & History*, www.wvculture.org/history/archives/blacks/timeline.html.

"A West Virginia Timeline," jeff560.tripod.com/wv-hist.html.

"Child Labor Pamphlet No. 86, National Child Labor Committee. Child Labor in West Virginia, by E. N. Clopper, 1908." *West Virginia Archives & History*, www.wvculture.org/history/labor/childlabor05.html.

"Civil War Heritage Park." *Welcome to Camp Nelson*, www.campnelson.org/home.htm.

"Civil War Union Militia Correspondence." *Child of the Rebellion: West Virginia Sesquicentennial Civil War Union Militia Correspondence*, www.wvculture.org/history/wvmemory/militia/gilmer/gilmer08a-03t.html.

"Coketon and Henry G. Davis" - Excerpt from *A Report of the West Virginia Institute for The History of Technology and Industrial Archaeology*, 1994. 12 Aug. 2006, www.jrclifford.org/images/PioneerPressCentEdition.pdf.

"Death of Henry Gassaway Davis." *West Virginia Archives & History*, www.wvculture.org/history/government/davishenry02.html.

"Dent, Marshall Mortimer." *Education @ LVA*, www.edu.lva.virginia.gov/.

"Frederick Douglass at Harpers Ferry." *National Park Service*, U.S. Department of the Interior, 10 Apr. 2015, www.nps.gov/hafe/learn/historyculture/frederick-douglass-at-harpers-ferry.htm.

"Friends of Blackwater." Newsletter - *Blackwater Heroine Carrie Williams – Her Story Shared by Her Descendants*, October 2014, p. 4. & *Historic Rose Hill Cemetery*, March 2017.

"Friends of Blackwater." Brochure - *West Virginia Central & Pittsburgh Railroad and Henry Gassaway Davis's Legacy.* http://saveblackwater.org/documents/August2017forweb.pdf

"Friends of Blackwater," Brochure - *Walking Tour of Thomas, West Virginia.* friendsofblackwater.org/index.html.

"Henry Gassaway Davis." *West-Virginia-Encyclopedia-Text*, www.wvencyclopedia.org/articles/1711.

"History." *Hillsdale College*, www.hillsdale.edu/about/history/.

"History Inside Pictures." *Monongah Coal Mine Photographs and History*, www.historyinsidepictures.com/Pages/MonongahCoalMinePhotographsandHistory.aspx.

"History Inside Pictures." *Monongah Mine Disaster Tombstones*, www.historyinsidepictures.com/Pages/MonongahMineDisasterTombstonesinlocalgraveyardsorcemeteries.aspx.

"History of West Virginia Mineral Industries - Coal." *WVGES Geology: History of West Virginia Coal Industry*, www.wvgs.wvnet.edu/www/geology/geoldvco.htm

"J. R. Clifford." *West Virginia Archives & History*, www.wvculture.org/history/archives/blacks/clifford.html.

"J.R. Clifford at Niagara." Excerpt from *W.E.B. Du Bois: Biography of a Race, 1868-1919*, by David Levering Lewis, 1993. *Pioneer Press – The Souvenir Edition*. 2004-2006, www.jrclifford.org/images/JR%20Clifford%20and%20the%20Carrie%20Williams%20Case.pdf. p. 24.

Libraries, WVU. "WVU Libraries." *News / WVU Libraries*, news.lib.wvu.edu/2014/08/18/j-r-clifford-and-the-pioneer-press/.

"Marshall Drama, Seminar to Honor State's First Black Lawyer." *West Virginia Record*, 12 Oct. 2007, wvrecord.com/stories/510592885-marshall-drama-seminar-to-honor-state-s-first-black-lawyer.

"Mining Disasters - An Exhibition 1907 Fairmont Mining Disaster." *https://Arlweb.msha.gov/DISASTER/MONONGAH/MONON11.asp*.

"Monograph Pictures and History." *Rare History and Ancient Technology Inside Pictures*, www.historyinsidepictures.com/.

"Ohio Memory, A Product of the Ohio History Connection and the State Library of Ohio." www.ohiomemory.org/.

"Pinecrest; Kerens, Richard C. House." *West Virginia Division of Culture and History. National Register of Historic Places - United States Department of Interior,* www.wvculture.org/shpo/nr/pdf.

"Reese L. Blizzard." www.findagrave.com/cgi-in/fg.cgi?page=gr&GRid=23853606.

"Remarkable Career of the Late Henry Gassaway Davis." *B and O Magazine*, vol. 3, 1914. pp. 38-45.

"Storer College Catalog 1869." *West Virginia Archives & History,* www.wvculture.org/history/education/storercatalog1869.html. pp. 10-11.

"Storer College: It Was Here A Century Ago That the NAACP Took Its First Steps." *The Journal of Blacks in Higher Education*, vol. 51, 2006, pp. 21–22. www.jstor.org/stable/doi:4133672.

"The 1892 Civil Rights Case of Coketon, West Virginia." *Traveling 219: The Seneca Trail,* 15 Nov. 2014, www.traveling219.com/stories/deep-creek-lake-elkins/1892-civil-rights-case-coketon-west-virginia/.

"The J.R. Clifford Project." *The J.R. Clifford Project,* www.jrclifford.org/. *The Pioneer Press - Niagara Centennial Edition,* vol. 125, no. 1, 12 Aug. 2006.

The Southeastern Reporter, vol. 31, pp. 985–986. West Publishing Company, 1899.

"Thomas and Coketon, WV." *Coalcamp USA*, www.coalcampusa.com/nowv/potomac/thomas-coketon-wv/thomas-coketon-wv.htm.

"The United States Constitution." *The U.S. Constitution Online - USConstitution.net*, usconstitution.net/const.html.

Transcript of Interview with Ancella Bickley, June 21, 1992, for the Film "West Virginia." www.wvculture.org/history/wvmemory/filmtranscripts/wvbickley.htm.

"United States Census Bureau." *Department of Commerce*, www.commerce.gov/doc/us-census-bureau#4/37.91/-96.24

"United States Department of Labor." *Mine Safety and Health Administration (MSHA) / MSHA - Protecting Miners' Safety and Health Since 1978*, www.msha.gov/. *Slavery*. Vol. 1 & 7, Santa Barbara, Calif., ABC-CLIO, 1997.

"West Virginia Coal Facts." *West Virginia Office of Miners' Health Safety and Training*, 2002, www.wvminesafety.org/disaster.htm.

"West Virginia's Mine Wars." *West Virginia Archives & History*, www.wvculture.org/history/archives/minewars.html.

"West Virginia Population by Race." *West Virginia Archives & History*, www.wvculture.org/history/archives/teacherresouces/censuspopulationnrace.html.

"West Virginia Statehood." *West Virginia Archives & History*, www.wvculture.org/history//statehood.html.

Whipple Company Store & Museum, Tour. whipplecompanystore.com/ourstory.html.

Williams v. Fairfax District Decided Reports of Cases Argued and Determined in the Supreme Court of Appeals of West Virginia, pp. 199-203. Tribune Printing Company, Charleston, 1905.

"WV Mine Disasters 1884 to Present." *West Virginia Mine Disasters, West Virginia Office of Miners' Health Safety and Training*, 2002, www.wvminesafety.org/disaster.htm.

"WV Teacher and Civil Rights Hero." *The Revivalist*, therevivalist.info/wv-teacher-and-civil-rights-hero/.

****

Atkinson, George Wesley, and Alvaro Franklin Gibbens. *Prominent Men of West Virginia*. Wheeling, W. Va., W.L. Collin, 1890.

Atkinson, George Wesley. *Bench and Bar of West Virginia*. Virginia Lawbook Company, 1919.

Bickley, Ancella R. "African-American Education." *West Virginia Encyclopedia*, www.wvencyclopedia.org/articles/26.

Bickley, Ancella R. *Honoring Our Past: Proceedings of the First Three Conferences on West Virginia's Black History.* Charleston, WV, West Virginia Humanities Commission, 1991.

Blum, John M. *The National Experience: A History of the United States.* 6th ed., San Diego, New York, Chicago, Atlanta, Washington D.C., London, Sydney, and Toronto, Harcourt Brace Jovanovich, Inc., January 28, 1985.

Blum, John M. *The National Experience: A History of the United States.* 8th ed., San Diego, New York, Chicago, Atlanta, Washington D.C., London, Sydney, and Toronto, Harcourt Brace Jovanovich, Inc., January 2, 1993.

Browne, Allen. "Landmarks." *A Ghost Town in the Southwest Corner of Maryland*, 9, March, 2012, allenbrowne.blogspot.com/2012/03/upper-potomac-ghost-town-in-southwest.html.

Clements, Bill. "WV Book Team: A Piece of W.Va. History." *Charleston Gazette-Mail,* www.wvgazettemail.com/article/20150913/GZ05/150919916.

Dickinson, Jack L. "Confederate Soldiers in West Virginia." https://www.wvencyclopedia.org/articles/1499.

Doyle, James T. "Brakeman—Builder—Benefactor A Tribute to Henry Gassaway Davis, Who Began His Business Career on the Baltimore and Ohio." *B and O Magazine*, vol. 3, 1914. pp. 45-48.

Eggleston, Jane R. "History of West Virginia Mineral Industries - Coal." *WVGES Geology: History of West Virginia Coal Industry*, Sept. 1996, www.wvgs.wvnet.edu/www/geology/geoldvco.htm.

Engle, Stephen D. "Mountaineer Reconstruction: Blacks in the Political Reconstruction of West Virginia." *The Journal of Negro History*, vol. 78, no. 3, 1993, pp. 137–165. www.jstor.org/stable/doi:10.2307/2717642.

Evans, Willis Fryatt. *History of Berkeley County, West Virginia*. Bowie, MD, Heritage Books. 2007.

Fisher, Emma. "Storer College." *The Pioneer Press - Niagara Centennial Edition*, vol. 125, no. 1, 12 Aug. 2006. p. 5.

Finkelman, Paul, and J. Clay Smith. "Not Only the Judges' Robes Were Black: African-American Lawyers as Social Engineers." *Stanford Law Review*, vol. 47, no. 1, 1994, pp. 161–209. JSTOR, www.jstor.org/stable/1229224.

Frail, T. A. "The Trial of the Century That Wasn't ." *Smithsonian Magazine*, vol. 48, no. 2, May 2017, p. 18.

Gorn, Elliott J. *Mother Jones: the Most Dangerous Woman in America.* New York, Hill and Wang, 2001.

Gouge, Marilyn. "Joseph T. HOKE Biography - Berkeley County GenWeb." rootsweb.ancestry.com/~wvberkel/hokejosbi.html.

Gozdzik Ph.D, Gloria. "A Historic Resource for Storer College at Harpers Ferry, West Virginia." *Nps.gov/Parkhistory/online_books/Hafe/Storer.pdf,* Jan. 2002.

Green, James R. *The Devil Is Here in These Hills: West Virginia's Coal Miners and Their Battle for Freedom.* New York, NY, Grove Press, 2015.

Gunter, Donald W. *Education @ Library of Virginia,* www.lva.virginia.gov/public/dvb/.

Halderman, Lori. "Friends of Blackwater", Newsletter June, 2012. *Visit Historic Coketon.* p. 6.

Katz, Michael S. "A History of Compulsory Education Laws." *Fastback Series,* Vol. 75, Bicentennial Series, Phi Delta Kappa Foundation, 1976.

Lewis, Ronald L. *Marmaduke Dent,* 27 Dec. 2016, www.wvencyclopedia.org/print/Article/1882.

Lewis, Ronald L. "From Peasant to Proletarian: The Migration of Southern Blacks to the Central Appalachian Coalfields." *The*

Journal of Southern History, vol. 55, no. 1, Feb. 1989, pp. 77–102. www.jstor.org/stable/doi:10.2307/2209720.

Maxwell, Hu, and Hyde, H. Clay. *History of Tucker County, West Virginia: from the Earliest Explorations and Settlements to the Present Time; with Biographical Sketches of More than Two Hundred and Fifty of the Leading Men, and a Full Appendix of Official and Electional History; Also, an Account of the Rivers, Forests and Caves of the County.* Kingwood, WV, Preston Publishing Company, 1884.

Maxwell, Hu. *The History of Randolph County, West Virginia.* Morgantown, WV, The Acme Publishing Company, 1898.

Nutter, T. Thomas, *West Virginia: History, Progress and Development.* Parsons, W. Va., McClain Print. Co., 1906.

Podvia, Mark W. "Williams v. Board of Education of Fairfax District: Bringing a Long-Forgotten West Virginia Case to Life." *Unbound: A Review of Legal History and Rare Books Journal of the Legal History and Rare Books Series Interest Section of the American Association of Law Libraries*, vol. 8, 2015, pp. 31–34.

Pepper, Charles M. *The Life and Times of Henry Gassaway Davis.* New York, NY, The Century Co., 1920.

Phillips, Cynthia A. *Images of Tucker County.* Charleston, SC, Arcadia Publishing, 2005.

Reid, John Phillip. *An American Judge: Marmaduke Dent of West Virginia*. New York University Press, 1968.

Rice, Connie Park. "'Don't Flinch nor Yield an Inch': J. R. Clifford and the Struggle for Equal Rights in West Virginia." *West Virginia History: A Journal of Regional Studies*, vol. 1, no. 2, 2008, pp. 45–68. www.jstor.org/stable/doi: 43264770.

Rice, Connie Park. "For Men and Measures: The Life and Legacy of Civil Rights Pioneer J.R. Clifford." *Eberly College of Arts and Sciences at West Virginia University*, 2007.

Rice, Connie Park. *J.R. Clifford: An African American National Biography*. Edited by Henry Louis Gates and Evelyn Brooks Higginbotham, vol. 2, Harvard and Oxford Press, 2008.

Rice, Donald L. *Randolph 200:A Bicentennial History of Randolph County, West Virginia: a Pictorial and Documentary Sampler*. Walsworth Publishing Company, 1987. Third Printing, 1999.

Riley, Thomas S. *Reports of Cases Determined by the Supreme Court of Appeals of West Virginia*, vol. 39, pp. 555–560. 1905. B.J.W. Printers, 1905.

Rodd, Thomas W. "Bringing the Story of J.R. Clifford to a 21st Century Audience." 12 Aug. 2006, www.jrclifford.org/images/PioneerPressCentEdition.pdf. p. 2.

Rodd, Thomas W. "J.R. Clifford, Esq., Heroic West Virginia Attorney and Civil Rights Pioneer." *The Advocate*, West Virginia Trial Lawyers Association, 2006, pp. 17–19.

Rodd, Thomas W. *Stories from West Virginia's Civil Rights History: A New Home for Liberty: J.R. Clifford and the Carrie Williams Case*. Charleston, WV, Quarrier Press, 2015.

Rodriguez, Junius P. *The Historical Encyclopedia of World Slavery*. Vol. 1 & 7, Santa Barbara, Calif., ABC-CLIO, 1997.

Rucker, Edgar P. *Reports of Cases Argued and Determined in the Supreme Court of Appeals of West Virginia*, vol. 45, pp. 199–203. Tribune Company Press, 1898.

Siebert, Wilbur H. "Light on the Underground Railroad." *The American Historical Review*, vol. 1, no. 3, 1896, pp. 455–463. www.jstor.org/stable1833723doi:10.2307/1833723.

Simmons, William J. *Men of Mark: Eminent, Progressive, and Rising*. Cleveland, OH, George M. Powell & Co., 1887.

Smith, Douglas C. "A West Virginia Dilemma: Martin v. Board of Education, 1896." *WV Division of Culture and History*, vol. 40, no. 2, 1979, pp. 158–163.

Smith, Lawrence. "Starcher Keeping Memory of State's First Black Attorney Alive." *West Virginia Record*, 5 Oct. 2006, wvrecord.com/stories/510589339-newsinator-starcher-keeping-memory-of-state-s-first-black-attorney-alive.

Spargo, John. *The Bitter Cry of the Children.* New York, The Macmillan Co. 1906.

Surrency, Erwin C. *The American Journal of Legal History/ A Review of An American Judge: Marmaduke Dent of West Virginia,* vol. 13, no. 4, 1969, pp. 395–398.

Steelhammer, Rick. "Play Tells Story of West Virginia's Statehood." *Charleston Gazette-Mail,* Associated Press, 31 Mar. 2011, ww.wvgazettemail.com/ap/ApTopStories/201103310363.

Teems, Katie. *Remembering the Fight for Civil Rights in Coketon.* 1 Feb. 2017, www.newhistoricthomas.com.

Wolfe, Eugene. "December 6, 1907 - No Christmas at Monongah". *Goldenseal* Vol. 19, No. 4, West Virginia Traditional Life Winter. 1993. pp. 9-15.

Woodson, C. G. "Early Negro Education in West Virginia." *The Journal of Negro History,* vol. 7, no. 1, Jan. 1922, pp. 23–63. www.jstor.org/stable/2713579doi:10.2307/2713579.

Index

Adams, Francis A. 121
Allen, W.B. 146
American Federation of
   Labor 44, 59
Arthur, Chester A. 32
Atkinson, George Wesley
   75
Atlanta Compromise 81,
   129
Backbone Mountain 34
Baltimore & Ohio Railroad
   20, 21, 24, 27, 38, 46
Battelle, Gordon 9-10
*Battle Hymn of the
   Republic* 81
Battle of Blair Mountain 62-
   63, 82
Bayard, Thomas 33
Bennedetto, R.D. 146
Berkeley Union 74
Bickley, Ancella 79, 97, 170
Black Fork 34
Blackwater Canyon 34
Blaine, James 33
Blizzard, Bill 62-63
Blizzard, Reese 60
Bluefield State College 78,
   94-95
Boreman, Arthur I. 12, 74

Brackett, Nathan 76, 77, 78,
   124
Brown, John 3-4, 14, 62, 80,
   81
Brown, Linda 112
*Brown vs. Board of
   Education of Topeka,
   Kansas* 78, 112-113,
   133, 173
Bruce, Blanche 110
Buxton and Landstreet
   Company Store 55, 102
Calhoun, John 22
Camp Nelson 121-124
Campbell, Archibald 10, 13
Carlile, John S. 6
Carnegie, Andrew 38
Carter, Emory Rankin 115
Chafin, Don 62
Chalfant, Francis 165
Chase, Salmon P. 9
Checkweighman 53
Chesapeake & Ohio Railway
   47
Children's Crusade 53
Chillicothe, Ohio 96-97,
   99-100
Civil Rights Act of 1875 49,
   111
Clay, Henry 22, 23, 37

Clifford, Isaac 119
Clifford, James Hensom 149
Clifford, John Robert 80, 81, 82, 83, 92, 99, 103, 111, 117-137, 148, 149, 150, 152, 153, 154, 155, 158-163, 166-170, 172-173
Clifford, Mary 81
Clifford, Mary Franklin 124
Clifford, Mary Satilpa 119
Clifford, Paul Ingram 119
Coal & Coke Railroad 36
Coal & Iron Railroad 36
Coketon vii, 53, 54, 57, 98, 147, 181
Coketon Colored School vii, 55, 94, 101-102, 147-148, 150, 153-154, 181
Colburn, S.E. 89
Company Scrip 52
Compromise of 1850 23, 98
Compromise of 1877 30, 48, 109-110
Confederate States of America 4
Constitutional Convention of West Virginia 8
Credo 81
Cribbing 52

Cromwell, John Wesley 125, 126
Curtain, Mrs. 120
Cuthbert, Stanley 88
Dackiewicz, Wladyslaw 36, 47
Davis, Caleb 20-21
Davis Coal and Coke Company viii, 19, 35, 36, 47, 50, 53, 54, 55, 57, 101, 146-147, 152, 159-161
Davis, Henry Gassaway 19-38, 46, 47, 50, 51, 53, 55, 75, 98, 101, 146
Davis, Jefferson 13
Davis, Katherine Bantz 24
Davis, Louisa 20, 21
Davis, Thomas Beall 25, 34, 50, 146
Davis, William 25, 27
Dayton, A.G. 150-151
Debs, Eugene 59
Democratic National Conventions 30, 31
Dent, Marmaduke 133, 162, 163-166, 167-170
Dent, Marshall 163-164
Douglas, Stephen 120, 163

Douglass, Frederick 11, 72, 80, 121
Douglass, Margaret 88
Du Bois, W.E.B. 81, 82, 99, 117, 136, 148
Dunn, Ransom 72
Edmunds, George H. 15
Edwards, Jacob 95, 100
Edwards, Rachel 95, 100
Elkins, Stephen B. 32, 33, 36, 38, 126
Engle, Stephen 91
Evans, George F. 126
Everett, Edward 72
Fair Labor Standards Act 65
Fairchild, E.B. 72, 77
Fairfax, Thomas, Sixth Lord 27
Fairmont Coal Company Mining Disaster 45, 56, 57, 65
Faulkner, E. Boyd 132
Fee, John G. 123
Feely and Wilson 146
Fifteenth Amendment 12, 13, 29, 71, 75
Finkelman, Paul 116, 129
First Wheeling Convention 7
Fleming, A. Brooks 57
Flick Amendment 13, 14, 29
Flick, W.H.H. 30, 127, 128, 132
Fort Monroe 13
Fort Sumter 4
Fossett, Ann-Elizabeth 99
Fourteenth Amendment 113, 130, 133, 149, 160, 162, 172
Franklin, Benjamin 20
Freedman's (Freeman's) Bureau 91
Freewill Baptists 72, 75, 76, 77
Fugitive Slave Law 24, 98
Furguson, Thomas 89, 91
Garfield, James A. 32
Geisbergers 146
Gibbens, Alvaro Franklin 75
Glasscock, William 60
Gompers, Samuel 59
Gorman, Arthur 33
Grandfather clause 48, 111
Grant, Ulysses S. 122, 124
Greeley, Horace 14
Green, Doris 94
Green, Israel 4

Green, James 27, 45
Guiteau, Charles 32
H.G. Davis & Company 25
Hall, Granville Davisson 6, 7, 13
Hall, Theron 123
Hammer vs. Dagenhart 65
Harding, Warren G. 62
Harper's Ferry 3
Harrison, Benjamin 32
Hatfield, Henry 60
Hatter, Hamilton 127
Healy, John J. 119, 121
Healy, Nellie 119
Helper, H. 5
Hershaw, L.M. 82
Hicks, Charles 89
Hillsdale College 72
Hoke, Joseph Hatcher 12, 71-84, 100, 121, 153-154, 155, 159, 160, 161, 169
Hope, John 81
Howard, George 21
Howe, Julia Ward 81
Huntington, Collis P. 47
Independent 74
Isaacs, Tucker 99
Jefferson, Thomas 46, 99

Jim Crow ix, 3, 48, 135, 171, 173
John Brown's Body 62, 81
Johnson, James Weldon 115
Jones, George 58
Jones, Mary Harris "Mother" 15, 58-60, 61, 62, 63, 65, 120
Keating-Owen Act 65
Keeney, Frank 61, 62
Kerens, Richard C. 33
Kern, John 60
Ku Klux Klan 101
La Sentinella del West Virginia 146
Lamb, Daniel 6
Lane, Frank 120
Lee, Robert E. 4, 74
"Let Up" Policy 29
Lien system 49
Lincoln, Abraham 4, 6, 11, 26
Lloyd, Henry Demarest 44
Lockwood House School 76-77
Logan, Rayford W. 172
Lynch, John Roy 125
Martin, Fenton 131
Martin, Louisiann 131
Martin, Nancy 131

Martin, Phillip 131
Martin, Rachel 131
Martin, Samuel 131
Martin, Thomas 131, 161, 162
Martin vs. Morgan County Board of Education 131-134, 161, 170
McClellan, George B. 12
McGan, William 146
McGuinn, Warner T. 115
McKinney, Richard 78
Meyer, Harold J. 150, 151-152, 155, 156, 158-159, 168
Mexican American War 23
Mexican Cession 23
Miner's Angel 15
Missouri Compromise 23
Mitchell, John 57-58
Montani Semper Liberi (Mountaineers Are Always Free) 15
Mooney, Fred 61, 62
Moore, John 88
Morgan, Ephraim 62
Mountain Echo 74
Murray, F.H.M. 82
National Bank of Davis 34

National Industrial Recovery Act 63
New York Tribune 14
Niagara Movement, Second Conference 81-82, 136, 172
Norfolk and Western Railroad 135
Nutter, Thomas Gillis 115, 146
Paint Creek-Cabin Creek Strike 60
Pan American Conferences 37
Pan-American Railroad Committee 37
Panic of 1837 21
Parker, Granville 9
Parkersburg Model 89
Party Boss 32
Peculiar Institution 1, 9
Pepper, Charles 20, 22
Piedmont Savings Bank 26
Pierpont, Francis 8, 74
Pioneer Press 117, 125-126, 128, 135, 149
Pitzer, U.S.G. 130
Plessy, Homer 112
Plessy vs. Ferguson 104, 112, 133, 162, 172, 173

Potomac and Piedmont Coal and Railway Company 28, 33
Procopio, Vincenzo 146
Protection Democrat 32
Pullman Strike 59
Radical Republicans, Radical Reconstruction 13, 30, 48, 110, 117
Raines vs. Chesapeake & Ohio Railway Company 166
Reid, John 166, 170
Republican National Conventions 83
Restored Government of Virginia 8, 9
Revels, Hiram 110
Rice, Connie Park 6, 103, 125, 128, 172
Rice, Donald 22
Riggs, William H. 128
Ritchie, Ellen 88
Roberts, D.W. 163
Roberts, Mary Caroline 163
Rodd, Thomas 155, 172
Roosevelt, Franklin Delano 63
Roosevelt, Theodore 31, 63, 165

Ruffner, Henry 5
Savage, Lon 62
Scott vs. Chesapeake & Ohio Railway Company 166
Second Wheeling Convention 8, 9, 89
Secret Six 14
Semi-Centennial Commission 37
Sergeant, William Smith 89, 91
Sharecropping 49
Sherman, William Tecumseh 122
Siebert, Wilbur 99
Simmons, Robert W. 89
Smith, Curtis 96
Smith, Gerrit 13
Social Darwinism 2
Social engineer 116, 129
Spargo, John 64
State of Kanawha 8
Stealey, John 76
Storer College 71, 75-81, 83, 92, 124, 155
Storer, John 77
Strauder vs. West Virginia 130, 153
Strawn, Silas N. 115

Strieby, C.O. 149, 154, 156-159, 167
Sumner, Charles 9, 48, 90, 111, 112
Sumner School 90, 92, 93, 124
Swann, Thomas 26
Tallifero, James 126
Taylor, Euclid 115
Templeton, John 88
The Boston Guardian 99
The Gospel of Wealth 38
Thomas, Matthew 89
Thomas Record 146
Thomas, Robert 89, 91
Thomas Sentinel 146
Tompkins, Addie 59
Treaty of Guadalupe Hidalgo 23
Trotter, James 99
Trotter, William Monroe 81, 99, 136
Turner, Henry McNeal 125
Turner, Nat 88
Twain, Mark 115
U.S. Colored Troops 121-124
Underground Railroad 98
Union-Conservative Party 29

United Mine Workers of America 15, 53, 56, 57, 58, 61
University of Michigan 73
Vanderbilt, Cornelius 14
Vanorsdale, M.A. 131
Virginia Code of 1860 89, 119
Virginia Secession Convention 4, 6, 8
Virginia Slave Code of 1819 88
Virginia Weekly Star 163
Waldron, J. Milton 136
Warfield, William A. 123
Warren, Earl 113
Washington, Booker T. 81, 129, 130
Washington, George 45
Webster, Daniel 22, 24
West Virginia Central & Pittsburg Railroad (WVC&PRR) 19, 28, 33, 34, 35, 36, 47, 50, 101
West Virginia Department of Mines 44
West Virginia State University 78, 94-95
West Virginia University 30, 74, 164-165

Wheeling Intelligencer 6, 10, 13
White, Albert B. 37
White, D.A. 124
Whyte, William Pinkney 33
Willey Amendment 11
Willey, Waitman T. 12-13, 163
Williams, Abraham L. 101, 103, 149, 175
Williams, Benjamin 101
Williams, Ethel 101
Williams, Henrietta 101
Williams, Irving 101
Williams, Josephine 101
Williams, Juanita 101
Williams, May 101
Williams (Thompson), Nevada 101, 149
Williams, Robert 101
Williams, Russell 101
Williams vs. the Tucker County Board of Education of Fairfax District 12, 66, 71, 83, 101, 121, 131, 148, 153, 154, 167-170, 172-173, 174, 182
Williams, Wendell Phillips 101

Willibur, Captain 98
Wilson, Lafayette 89
Windom, William 33
Wisner, J. Nelson 127
Woodside, Dr. 21

About the Author

Kathleen Jackson Costantini has over twenty-five years experience as a teacher, administrator and academic advisor in diverse urban school settings. Throughout her career, she has developed and taught Advanced Placement courses in United States History and American Government and Politics. A specialist in the study of primary source documents, she was the director of a Gilder Lehreman Institute of American History enrichment program for high school students. Kathleen later founded the American Studies Writing Workshop, a tuition free document based writing program for low income students in New York.

Kathleen is a guest lecturer at Manhattan College where she has taught graduate classes in Professional Writing and

Counseling the College Applicant. She is the co-author of *Counseling 21st Century Students for Optimal College and Career Readiness* (Routledge Press). Currently, Kathleen is an educational counselor and consultant assisting students with various educational needs, including learning differences, organizational issues and developmental writing skills. Most importantly, she is a writer avidly exploring topics in American history.

Kathleen earned her B.A. in English Literature at the University of Detroit and her M. A. in English Literature at Fordham University. She lives in New York and is frequently in the Mountain State.

35th Star Publishing
www.35thstar.com

www.ingramcontent.com/pod-product-compliance
Lightning Source LLC
Chambersburg PA
CBHW071232080526
44587CB00013BA/1583